I0458906

The New Paradigm: Conscious Healing In The Age Of Ai
Copyright © 2025 by Dr. Constance Santego.

All rights reserved. No part of this publication may be reproduced, distributed or transmitted in any form or by any means, including photocopying, recording, or other electronic or mechanical methods, without the prior written permission of the publisher, except in the case of brief quotations embodied in critical reviews and certain other noncommercial uses permitted by copyright law. For permission requests, write to the publisher, addressed "Attention: Permissions Coordinator," at the address below.

Copy Editor & Interior Design: Constance Santego
Book Layout: ©2017 BookDesignTemplates.com

Ordering Information:
Quantity sales. Special discounts are available on quantity purchases by corporations, associations, and others. For details, contact the "Special Sales Department" at the address above.

Trade Paperback ISBN: 978-1-997907-00-8
Ebook ISBN 978-1-997907-01-5
Created and published In Canada. Printed and bound in the United States of America

First Edition
Published by Maximillian Enterprises
Kelowna, BC Canada
www.constancesantego.ca

The New Paradigm: Conscious Healing In The Age Of AI

How Coherence, Frequency, and Natural Intelligence
Redefine Health and Humanity

Dr. Constance Santego

Maximillian Enterprises
Kelowna, BC

Dedication

To every soul who has ever searched for the light —
only to discover it was shining within them all along.

To my students, clients, and fellow healers —
your courage to feel, to grow, and to transform
has been the greatest teacher of all.

To the scientists who dare to study the invisible,
and the visionaries who trust what cannot yet be proven —
you are building the bridge between worlds.

And to my husband, family, and loved ones —
thank you for grounding my dreams in love
and reminding me that coherence begins at home.

May this book awaken the remembrance
that you are not broken, not separate, not small —
you are the pulse of divine intelligence
breathing harmony into form.

This is for you —
the medicine, the messenger, and the miracle.

ALSO BY DR. CONSTANCE SANTEGO

NOVELS
Illegitimate Grace
Ashcroft Hollow

Okanagan Trilogy:
Beneath the Vineyards
Under the Okanagan Sun
Guardian of the Lake

The Nine Spiritual Gifts Series:
Journey of a Soul – (Vol 1 Michael)
Language of a Soul – (Vol 2 Gabriel)
Prophecy of a Soul – (Vol 3 Bath Kol)
Healing of a Soul – (Vol 4 Raphael)
Miracles of a Soul – (Vol 5 Hamied)
Knowledge of a Soul – (Vol 6 Raziel)
Wisdom of a Soul – (Vol 7 Uriel)
Faith of a Soul – (Vol 8 Pistis Sophia)

NONFICTION
The Intuitive Life, The Gift Of Prophecy, Third Edition
Fairy Tales, Dreams And Reality… Where Are You On Your Path?
Second Edition
Your Persona… The Mask You Wear
Archangel Michael's Soul Retrieval Guide
Tesla And The Future Of Energy Medicine
Beyond Tesla: Advancing The Science Of Energy Healing
Tesla's Code: Mastering Energy, Frequency, And Creative Power
Beyond The Mind: Harnessing The Power Of Astral Projection For
Creative Awakening
Bend, Don't Break: Finding Your Way Back To Abundance
Ring Therapy: A Guide To Healing And Balance
Ring Therapy Pocket Guide
Floraopathy™: The Art And Science Of Vibrational Healing With
Essential Oils
Dear Older Me: A Memoir… Of Sorts
It's Just Like Poker: A Spiritual Guide To Playing The
Cards Life Deals You

Signs And Meanings: What The Feet Reveal About Health, Stress, And The Body's Story
Auricions: Unlocking Subconscious Healing Through Quantum Medicine
Quick Fix Acupressure Method
Manifestation – The DREAM Method in 5 Steps
Confidence- Mastering the Dream Method

REIKI WISDOM, SERIES:
Angelic Lifestyle, a Vibrant Lifestyle
Angelic Lifestyle 42-Day Energy Cleanse
Reiki and the Power of The Joint Points: Unlocking Energy Pathways for Healing (Vol I)
Reiki and Karmic Healing: Releasing Patterns From Past Lives (Vol II)
Reiki and the Five Elements (Vol III)
Secrets of a Healer, Magic Of Reiki
The Reiki Master's Manual

CHAKRA SERIES:
Heart Chakra 101: The Bridge
Root Chakra 101: Building Safety, Survival, Foundation
Sacral Chakra 101: Creativity, Pleasure, Emotions
Solar Plexus Chakra 101: Power, Confidence, Will
Throat Chakra 101: Truth, Voice, Self-Expression
Third Eye Chakra 101: Intuition, Vision, Insight
Crown Chakra 101: Spiritual Connection, Transcendence.

SECRETS OF A HEALER, SERIES:
Magic Of Aromatherapy (Vol I)
Magic Of Reflexology (Vol II)
Magic Of The Gifts (Vol III)
Magic Of Muscle Testing (Vol IV)
Magic Of Iridology (Vol V)
Magic Of Massage (Vol VI)
Magic Of Hypnotherapy (Vol VII)
Magic Of Reiki (Vol VIII)
Magic Of Advanced Aromatherapy (Vol IX)
Magic Of Esthetics (Vol X)
The Reiki Master's Manual (Vol XI)

ADULT COLORING JOURNALS
SERIES-ZEN COLORING:
Quantum Energy and Mindful Living Journal (Vol 1)
Reiki Energy Journal (Vol 2)
Nine Spiritual Gifts Journal (Vol 3)
I Forgive Journal (Vol 4)

FOR CHILDREN
I am Big Tonight. I Don't Need the Light
The Magic Elf Book: 25 Days of Surprises

COOKBOOK
My Favorite Recipes, with a Hint of Giggle

BUISNESS
How To Use ChatGPT For Authors: From Idea To Published Book
Scaling Beyond 6 Figures: Strategies For Health & Wellness Professionals
The Academypreneur's Playbook: Turn Knowledge Into A
Revenue-Generating School

HUMOR/GIFT BOOK
How Do You Like Your Eggs? **Crack Into Your Personality, Yolk and All**

Contents

The New Paradigm: Conscious Healing In The Age Of AI

How Coherence, Frequency, and Natural Intelligence Redefine Health and Humanity

Dr. Constance Santego

Author's Note — Why I Wrote This Book

By Dr. Constance Santego, Ph.D., DNM

We are entering an era unlike any before it — a time when machines can predict disease before symptoms appear, but they cannot feel the pulse of compassion or intuition that creates true healing. Artificial intelligence is transforming our outer world, yet it is our **natural intelligence** — the wisdom of energy, emotion, and consciousness — that must guide our inner one.

This book is about reclaiming that inner genius — the frequency of wholeness that no algorithm can replicate.

There comes a moment in every healer's journey when the techniques, tools, and even teachings begin to merge into something greater. For me, that moment arrived when I realized that all the systems I had studied, practiced, and taught for more than two decades — Reiki, chakras, vibrational medicine, intuition, Tesla's frequencies, the five elements, emotional healing, and beyond — were never separate at all.

They were simply different languages describing the same intelligence.

That intelligence is **energy** — the silent architect of life itself. The more I worked with it, the more I understood that healing isn't about fixing what's broken; it's about remembering our *original frequency* — the state of coherence between heart, mind, and soul where creation naturally flows.

Over the years, I've watched thousands of students and clients heal through this understanding. I have seen pain dissolve when a person touches one spot on their body and allows themselves to fully feel the emotion there — and then touches another spot while recalling joy, love, or gratitude. As the heart and mind reconnect through feeling and touch, the body recalibrates itself.

What science now calls *coherence* is, in essence, the **soul remembering harmony**.

When I first heard Tony Robbins speak about the heart and brain vibrating at the same rhythm to create transformation, something inside me sparked. I realized we were describing the same truth — the **energetic alignment** that unlocks human genius. It confirmed what I had been witnessing for years in my own practice: the real power of healing lies not in the mind alone, but in the marriage of **thought, emotion, and frequency**.

That discovery became my life's work — a way to merge the spiritual with the scientific, the ancient with the modern, the human with the divine.

This book, *The Zone of Healing Genius*, is the culmination of that realization — the unifying code behind every modality I've ever taught. It offers not just concepts but an *experience*: a way to feel coherence, to live it, and to sustain it in a rapidly changing world.

We stand at the threshold of a new evolution — not just of medicine, but of consciousness itself. As technology accelerates, humanity must evolve in balance, cultivating heart intelligence, emotional mastery, and energetic awareness. Healing is no longer about diagnosis or data; it is about **resonance** — aligning the frequencies of the body, mind, and soul so that life itself flows effortlessly again.

I wrote this book because I believe every person carries this genius within them. My hope is that as you read, you will not only understand energy — you will *feel* it. You will awaken your own coherence — the intelligence of your body, the wisdom of your soul, and the light that has been waiting patiently to shine.

Welcome to your **Zone of Healing Genius.**
The world is ready for your frequency.

— *Dr. Constance Santego*

"Artificial Intelligence will analyze the body. Natural Intelligence will harmonize the soul. The New Paradigm is where they meet."

What Is the New Paradigm?

For centuries, healing followed the **old paradigm** — a mechanistic model that treated the body like hardware, separate from mind, emotion, and spirit. Illness was seen as malfunction, and medicine sought to fix parts in isolation.

But humanity is awakening to a **new paradigm** — one that views the body as living software: intelligent, dynamic, and programmable through frequency, thought, and emotion.

In the old paradigm, healing meant removing symptoms.
In the new paradigm, healing means restoring *coherence* — the natural harmony between the heart, brain, and biofield that allows the body's systems to self-correct.

This shift unites **science and spirit**, **data and intuition**, and **artificial and natural intelligence**. It's not about rejecting technology but remembering that energy, emotion, and consciousness are the original operating system of life.

"The old paradigm treats the body as hardware.
The new paradigm understands it as software — programmable through frequency and emotion."

The New Paradigm invites you to live as an integrated field of awareness — where biology meets light, where technology mirrors consciousness, and where healing is no longer something done *to* you, but something awakened *through* you.

Why This Book Is Different

Most books teach how to heal.
Few teach how to evolve — *with* the very technologies that are reshaping our world.

We stand at a turning point in human consciousness. Artificial Intelligence is transforming how we understand data, health, and even thought itself. But while machines can analyze the patterns of life, only consciousness can *rewrite* them.

The New Paradigm: Conscious Healing in the Age of AI bridges two worlds once thought to be opposites — the ancient and the futuristic, the intuitive and the analytical, the spiritual and the scientific.

This book unites:

- The timeless wisdom of **Reiki, chakras, and vibrational medicine**,
- With the frontier of **AI-assisted biofield mapping, coherence tracking, and consciousness research.**

It speaks to both the **seeker of spirit** and the **student of science**, offering not a new method, but a new way of *being* — one that harmonizes natural and artificial intelligence into coherence.

"The future of healing isn't human versus machine —
it's consciousness guiding technology through love."

This work marks the dawn of a new genre — **Conscious Medicine** — where healing is no longer seen as repair, but as resonance.
You are not just learning to heal; you are learning to evolve.
Welcome to the bridge between energy and evolution.

Preface: The Bridge Between Two Intelligences

We are living in the greatest leap of evolution humanity has ever known.

For the first time, our creations — the algorithms, sensors, and circuits we have built — are beginning to think, learn, and mimic the patterns of life itself.

Artificial Intelligence has become our mirror, reflecting back the brilliance and the blindness of human consciousness.

Yet beyond the code lies another form of intelligence — older, infinite, and organic.

It beats in the rhythm of the heart, hums through the neural pathways of the body, and vibrates in every cell that has ever known life.

It does not compute. It *resonates.*

It does not predict. It *feels.*

This is **Natural Intelligence** — the living field of awareness that connects all beings to the greater intelligence of the universe.

For centuries, mystics and scientists have circled this truth from different directions.

Tesla spoke of energy, frequency, and vibration as the keys to understanding the universe.

Turing unlocked the logic of intelligence through mathematics and machine.

Today, their visions converge.

AI gives us the tools to see energy as data, to map emotion as pattern, to quantify coherence as frequency.

But no machine, however advanced, can generate the heartbeat of compassion, the warmth of touch, or the intuitive knowing that transcends words.

These belong to the realm of Natural Intelligence — consciousness embodied, love made measurable.

The purpose of this book is not to choose between the two, but to unite them.
To awaken a healing paradigm where technology amplifies wisdom, where data serves compassion, and where human coherence becomes the new source code of evolution.

When Artificial and Natural Intelligence stand as allies rather than opposites, a bridge is formed — one that connects science and spirit, body and soul, human and divine.
That bridge is you.

Welcome to *The New Paradigm.*
Welcome to *The Bridge Between Two Intelligences.*

PART I – THE NEW PARADIGM OF HEALING

You can't heal from the same frequency that created the imbalance.

1 | The Pattern Code

Close your eyes for a moment.
Imagine you're standing in a room filled with mirrors. Each one reflects a different part of your life—relationships, health, money, purpose. Now picture a faint vibration running through the air, the steady hum of your thoughts and feelings echoing back at you. Some mirrors shimmer with light; others ripple with distortion. Those ripples are your **patterns**.

Patterns aren't random habits or personality quirks. They are **energetic programs**—vibrations recorded through emotion, belief, and experience that repeat until they're rewritten. Every time you feel an emotion, your body releases a signature frequency. Every repeated emotion etches that frequency a little deeper into your cells, your nervous system, and your energy field. Over time, the signal becomes automatic: a loop.

When the same loop keeps running—fear, doubt, guilt, "I'm not enough"—it's like music played off-key. The body loses harmony, the mind loses clarity, and life begins to echo that discord. Healing begins the moment you can *see* the loop, *feel* its texture in your body, *hear* its rhythm in your thoughts, and *know* you have the power to change the sound.

Seeing the Pattern

Notice what keeps showing up. The same argument, symptom, or setback? Patterns reveal themselves through repetition. Awareness is the first disruption.

Feeling the Pattern

Where does it live in your body? A tight throat, a clenched jaw, a heavy chest? Sensation is the body's way of saying, "Energy is stuck here." When you touch that place with presence instead of resistance, the loop begins to loosen.

Hearing the Pattern

Every pattern speaks in inner dialogue:
"I always mess this up." "No one listens." "I'm too old to start over." Listen without judgment. You can't change the frequency of a song you refuse to hear.

Knowing the Pattern

This is the turning point—realizing the pattern isn't *you*. It's simply energy replaying history. The moment you know that truth, you're already raising your vibration above the loop.

EXERCISE – PATTERN AWARENESS SCAN

1. Sit quietly. Place one hand on your heart and one on your solar plexus.
2. Recall a recurring frustration or emotion.
3. Ask yourself: *Where do I feel it? What words or memories rise with it?*
4. Now breathe deeply and imagine that frequency as color or sound.
5. Visualize adjusting the tone—brighter, softer, harmonious— until your body feels calm.

You've just begun to rewrite your code.

How Old Survival Patterns Create Energetic "Static"

Every human being carries a library of ancient instructions — codes written in the language of survival. Long before you learned to speak or think, your body learned to adapt. When something felt unsafe, it tightened muscles, shifted breath, flooded your system with adrenaline, and created an energetic blueprint that said: *"Remember this. Protect yourself next time."*

Those early protections were wise at the time; they kept you alive, emotionally or physically. But when those same patterns continue to run long after the danger has passed, they become energetic **static** — background noise that interferes with your natural frequency of coherence.

Think of your energy field as an orchestra: the heart is percussion, the mind the strings, the emotions the winds. A survival pattern is like a musician who never stops playing the same anxious note. It drowns out harmony. The body tenses. The mind narrows. Breath shortens. Even if life is calm, the nervous system acts as if the storm never ended.

This static shows up in subtle ways:

- You overthink every choice because your system learned that mistakes aren't safe.
- You shrink your voice because long ago, speaking truth invited conflict.
- You over-give and under-receive because love once felt conditional.
- You keep busy to outrun stillness, because stillness once felt like danger.

Each of these patterns hums just beneath awareness. You might not hear them directly, but you feel the interference: fatigue, confusion, self-doubt, physical pain. It's the noise between you and your natural clarity.

HOW THE STATIC FORMS

1. **Emotional Imprint:** Every intense emotion leaves a frequency in your field. Fear, shame, anger — all carry distinct energetic tones.
2. **Repetition:** Each time the emotion replays, the signal strengthens, carving neural and energetic pathways.
3. **Association:** The brain begins to link unrelated situations to the original trigger.
4. **Automatic Response:** The body reacts before thought — fight, flight, freeze, or appease — and the static becomes constant background hum.

RECOGNIZING THE STATIC IN YOUR FIELD

You'll know a survival pattern is active when your reaction feels bigger than the moment. Your mind says, *"It's not a big deal,"* but your body feels as if it is. That mismatch between reality and reaction is energetic residue. It distorts the communication between your heart and brain — the very coherence required for healing and creation.

CLEARING THE STATIC

You cannot force it silent; you must *re-tune* it.
Start with awareness. When you feel the surge — the tightness, the rush, the shutdown — pause and name it:

"This is an old frequency trying to protect me."

Place a hand where you feel it most strongly. Breathe. Then bring your other hand to your heart and recall a moment of genuine safety or love. Alternate your attention between the two sensations. With each cycle, imagine the static softening, the sound smoothing into harmony.

That's how coherence begins: not by erasing your past, but by teaching your energy that safety exists *now*.

Survival patterns are not enemies; they are echoes. When you listen to them consciously, they reveal the story your body has been trying to finish for years. And when you offer them new rhythm — calm breath, present awareness, compassion — the noise fades. What remains is stillness.

And in that stillness, your true frequency — your genius — comes through, clear as music.

RECOGNIZING YOUR TOP FIVE PATTERNS

(The Healer's Wound, The Over-Thinker, The Not-Enough, The Hidden Anger, and The Fear of Visibility)

Before you can rewrite a pattern, you have to see it for what it is— not a flaw, but a frequency you've been transmitting for years. Each of these five archetypal patterns hides a brilliant quality underneath the distortion. When you recognize them, you begin to reclaim the energy trapped inside them.

1. The Healer's Wound – "I can help everyone but myself."

You give endlessly. You sense pain in others as if it were your own. You've built a life around mending, soothing, fixing.
But deep underneath is an old contract: *If I keep healing others, maybe my own pain will finally rest.*

This creates energetic leakage—your field spreads outward, leaving your center unguarded.

Reframe: Your empathy is sacred, but healing begins inward. When your frequency is coherent, your presence alone becomes medicine.

Feel it: Place a hand over your heart and whisper, *"My wholeness heals more than my effort ever could."*

2. The Over-Thinker – "If I can just figure it out, I'll be safe."

The mind races to solve everything—every symptom, every emotion, every uncertainty.

It's brilliant but exhausting, like trying to surf a tidal wave with logic alone.

This pattern forms when the nervous system equates control with safety. The head takes command, and the body's wisdom goes silent.

Reframe: Thinking is not the enemy; ungrounded thinking is.

Feel it: Breathe into your belly. Ask, *"What does my body already know that my mind keeps overriding?"*

When thought meets breath, clarity replaces noise.

3. The Not-Enough – "I have to earn my worth."

No matter how much you learn, give, or achieve, it never feels sufficient.

This pattern hums with the frequency of scarcity—a leftover vibration from times you were unseen or unvalidated.

Energetically, it compresses the solar plexus, dimming confidence and willpower.

Reframe: Worth is not currency; it's current. It flows when you allow, not when you strive.

Feel it: Place your palm just below your ribs. Breathe into that space until you sense expansion. Whisper, *"I am already enough; I'm simply remembering."*

4. The Hidden Anger – "I'm fine."

Anger often hides beneath spirituality, kindness, or professionalism. You learned early that expressing it led to conflict or rejection, so you turned it inward.

Energetically, suppressed anger becomes heat—digestive issues, jaw tension, insomnia.

Reframe: Anger is not destructive; it's directive energy asking for motion.

Feel it: Let the body move—shake, stretch, exhale with sound. Say, *"It's safe to release energy; I don't need to hold it anymore."*

When anger flows, it transforms into clarity and strength.

5. The Fear of Visibility – "It's safer to stay small."

You sense the greatness inside you but hesitate to show it.

This pattern often hides under humility or self-protection. In truth, it's the residue of ancestral memories where shining drew danger or judgment.

Energetically, it constricts the throat and heart, lowering your broadcast signal.

Reframe: Visibility is not exposure—it's resonance. The world needs the vibration you carry.

Feel it: Touch your throat lightly, inhale through your nose, and exhale while imagining your voice as light filling the room. Whisper, *"It's safe to be seen in my truth."*

Integrating the Awareness

Each pattern is a teacher. Together they form the curriculum of your evolution.

Recognizing them is not about self-critique—it's about *energetic literacy.*

You are learning to read your own frequency map: where energy leaks, where it flows, and where it's waiting to be reclaimed.

The moment you name a pattern without judgment, its vibration begins to loosen.

And as those frequencies shift, coherence—your natural genius state—emerges from underneath, steady and luminous.

QUICK PRACTICE: INTERRUPT THE LOOP — ONE BREATH + ONE TOUCH

Every pattern has a rhythm — a predictable pulse of emotion and thought. To break it, you don't need hours of meditation; you only need a single moment of conscious interruption.

One breath. One touch. One shift of frequency.

This simple technique brings coherence back to your field in less than a minute.

Try it now — through the four intuitive channels of perception.

1. The Visual Channel – "See it shift."

Purpose: For those who process energy through imagery and light.

1. Close your eyes and picture the pattern — a color, shape, or movement in your body.
2. Inhale deeply and imagine golden light entering through the crown of your head.
3. Place your hand gently on the part of your body where the pattern feels strongest.
4. As you exhale, *see* that light flooding the area, dissolving static, turning the image clear.
5. Whisper internally: *"I see harmony returning."*
   What you see becomes the signal you send.

2. The Feeler Channel – "Feel it change."

Purpose: For those who sense energy through touch, emotion, or bodily sensation.

1. Notice where the tension, heaviness, or pulse lives inside you.
2. Take one slow, full breath.
3. Place a hand there — not to fix, just to acknowledge.
4. Feel the warmth of your palm meeting that energy.
5. With each breath, let comfort spread outward until the body softens.
6. Say to yourself: *"It's safe to feel this and let it flow."*
   What you feel is the doorway to release.

3. The Knower Channel – "Know it realigns."

Purpose: For those who process energy through intuition and insight.

1. Center your awareness behind your sternum — the seat of your inner knowing.
2. Inhale as you touch that point lightly with your fingertips.
3. Silently affirm: *"I know this pattern is only energy, and I command it back to balance."*
4. Exhale and sense a shift — subtle but definite — as truth replaces tension.
5. Imagine the energy reorganizing itself into order and peace.
   What you know with certainty becomes law in your field.

4. The Audio Channel – "Hear it harmonize."

Purpose: For those attuned to sound, rhythm, or inner dialogue.

1. Breathe in through your nose, exhale slowly through your mouth with an audible sigh.
2. Place one hand over your throat or heart — wherever your sound feels blocked.
3. Hum softly, or repeat a soothing word: "Peace," "Calm," "Light."
4. Feel the vibration move through your body.
5. Imagine the discordant "noise" of the pattern fading until only harmony remains.
   What you hear becomes the frequency you embody.

Integration: The One-Minute Reset

- **One breath:** reconnects heart and brain.
- **One touch:** grounds the energy in your body.
- **One channel:** activates your natural intelligence.

Use this practice anytime you feel caught in an old loop — anxiety rising, self-doubt cycling, energy draining.
Each time you breathe and touch with awareness, you're sending your nervous system a new message:

"I am safe. I am present. I am rewriting the code."

Repeat it often enough, and that moment of coherence becomes your new default state —
the first step into your **Zone of Healing Genius.**

2 | Emotion: The Fuel of Frequency

Emotion is the language your energy field uses to communicate with your body and your soul.

Close your eyes for a moment and remember the last time you felt pure joy — the kind that makes your chest expand and your breath lift. Now recall a moment of deep worry or anger — notice how the body contracts, breath shortens, and thought narrows.
That shift you just felt isn't imagination — it's energy.

Emotion is energy in motion.
Every feeling is a current — a measurable frequency that moves through your nervous system, your cells, and the invisible field surrounding you. When emotion flows freely, energy moves in harmony. When it's suppressed, resisted, or overamplified, energy becomes distorted.

This is the *fuel* of your frequency — the power source of your entire being.

WHERE SCIENCE AND ENERGY MEDICINE MEET

Modern **neuroscience** and **Reiki** may use different languages, but they describe the same phenomenon.

Neuroscience says:

Every emotion begins as a *chemical message*.
Neurotransmitters and hormones such as dopamine, serotonin, and cortisol flood the body in response to perception.
These chemicals alter heartbeat, digestion, muscle tone, and even gene expression.
When emotions are processed, the nervous system returns to equilibrium; when repressed, those chemicals linger, keeping the body in chronic stress.

Reiki and energy medicine say:

Emotions are *vibrational currents* in the auric and chakra systems.
When energy flows smoothly through these centers, the field emits balanced frequencies.
When emotion is held or denied, stagnation appears as blockages — dense vibrations that mirror dis-ease before it manifests physically.

Different language, same truth: **energy that moves heals; energy that stagnates hurts.**

THE BRIDGE BETWEEN BRAINWAVES AND BREATH

Each emotion corresponds to a rhythm — a literal vibration measurable by science:

- Calm produces slow, coherent heart rhythms.
- Love and gratitude generate synchronized alpha brainwaves.
- Fear and anger create erratic patterns and shallow breathing.

Your **breath** is the bridge. Every inhale and exhale adjusts the electromagnetic conversation between your heart and brain.
This is where coherence lives — when emotion, breath, and energy align in rhythm.

When you breathe with awareness, you're not just calming your mind; you're recalibrating your entire frequency field.

EMOTIONAL FLOW IN REIKI TERMS

Reiki teaches that energy follows thought and intention.
If thought is the blueprint, *emotion is the current* that animates it.
When you send healing energy through the hands, it travels along emotional pathways — love, compassion, peace.
The more authentic the feeling, the stronger the flow.

That's why mechanical Reiki (going through the motions) feels weak, while heartfelt Reiki (feeling the energy) radiates power.
Emotion is the voltage that turns subtle energy into transformation.

THE SPECTRUM OF EMOTION AND FREQUENCY

Emotion	Frequency Vibration	Physiological State	Energy Medicine View
Love / Gratitude	High, coherent	Open, expansive	Healing, harmonizing
Joy / Peace	High, stable	Regulated heart rate	Integration, flow
Fear / Anger	Low, chaotic	Adrenal activation	Blocked, dissonant
Shame / Guilt	Dense, slow	Collapsed posture	Energy depletion

You can't eliminate low emotions — they are part of the spectrum of human experience — but you can *transmute* them by letting them move. The goal is not to feel only joy; it's to allow all energy to stay in motion.

PRACTICE – MOVING ENERGY THROUGH EMOTION

1. **Identify the feeling.**
   Name it out loud or silently. Naming anchors it into awareness.
2. **Locate it.**
   Where does it live in your body? Chest, gut, jaw, throat?
3. **Breathe through it.**
   Inhale slowly, exhale longer than you inhale.
4. **Visualize motion.**
   Imagine the emotion as color or light swirling gently, then expanding outward until it dissolves.
5. **Reframe.**
   Ask: *What is this emotion trying to move or teach me?*

Repeat until the emotion feels lighter, or until you sense warmth, clarity, or even subtle tingling — signs of energy flow returning.

ENERGETIC INSIGHT

Emotions are not obstacles to healing — they *are* the healing.
They carry information from the soul to the body, and when honored, they guide you back into alignment.
Suppressing emotion is like damming a river; acknowledging it allows the water to purify itself.

When emotion moves, energy flows.
When energy flows, coherence returns.
And when coherence returns — **you remember who you are**: a symphony of frequencies perfectly tuned to life itself.

The Chemistry of Coherence vs. Chaos

Your body is a living laboratory — every thought and emotion releases chemistry into your bloodstream. The molecules that circulate are the echoes of your inner frequency.

When your **energy is coherent**, your entire system speaks one harmonious language. The heart, brain, hormones, and cells synchronize into rhythm — a biological symphony of clarity and flow. When your **energy is chaotic**, the communication scrambles. Signals misfire, hormones surge unevenly, and the body moves into defense mode rather than creation.

Let's explore what's happening in both states — not just energetically, but *chemically*.

"The next evolution of intelligence is not artificial or natural — it's integrative."

COHERENCE: CHEMISTRY OF HARMONY

Coherence begins with a calm, rhythmic heartbeat.
That steady rhythm sends ordered electrical signals to the brain,
which responds by balancing neurotransmitters and hormones.
Your body literally bathes in harmony.

System	Coherent Chemistry	Effect on the Body
Nervous System	Parasympathetic dominance (rest–repair state)	Muscles relax, digestion improves, immune system activates
Endocrine System	Balanced release of oxytocin, serotonin, and endorphins	Feelings of love, peace, safety, and connection
Brainwaves	Alpha–theta synchronization	Heightened creativity, intuition, and focus
Heart Field	Smooth heart rate variability (HRV)	Emotional stability, reduced stress response
Cellular Response	Increased oxygenation and repair	Tissue rejuvenation, anti-inflammatory effects

When you feel gratitude, compassion, or joy, the heart sends a
coherent signal to the brain through the vagus nerve.
The brain interprets this as safety, releases feel-good chemistry, and
communicates that safety back to every organ.
It's a feedback loop of wellness — *emotion → energy → chemistry →
harmony.*

Coherence is not an idea; it's a measurable biochemical state of
peace.

CHAOS: CHEMISTRY OF DISTORTION

Chaos begins when the body senses threat — real or imagined.
The heart rhythm becomes erratic, sending inconsistent signals to the brain.
The brain, confused, releases a cocktail of stress hormones — adrenaline, norepinephrine, and cortisol.
This short-term survival chemistry is life-saving in danger but toxic in repetition.

System	Chaotic Chemistry	Effect on the Body
Nervous System	Sympathetic dominance (fight–flight–freeze)	Muscle tension, shallow breathing, digestive shutdown
Endocrine System	Excess cortisol and adrenaline	Chronic inflammation, hormonal imbalance
Brainwaves	Beta overactivity	Anxiety, overthinking, fragmented focus
Heart Field	Irregular heart rate variability	Emotional reactivity, exhaustion
Cellular Response	Oxidative stress, reduced immune defense	Fatigue, pain, accelerated aging

This is the chemistry of *energetic static* — when emotion is trapped and the body believes the past is still happening.
Your biology keeps broadcasting the vibration of survival even when your mind says, "I'm fine."

Chaos chemistry is what happens when emotion stops moving — when energy loses rhythm.

RECALIBRATING CHEMISTRY THROUGH ENERGY

Here's the empowering truth:
You can shift from chaos to coherence in under three minutes using breath, touch, and emotion.

1. **Breathe slowly** — five seconds in, five seconds out.
   This activates the vagus nerve and signals safety to the brain.
2. **Place your hand on your heart.**
   This simple gesture increases oxytocin, the bonding hormone.
3. **Recall a moment of gratitude or compassion.**
   Within 90 seconds, cortisol begins to drop, and serotonin rises.
4. **Visualize your cells lighting up with even rhythm.**
   Your electromagnetic field stabilizes; coherence becomes chemical reality.

Your body doesn't distinguish between a real and a remembered emotion — it responds to the *frequency* you hold.

THE COHERENCE EQUATION

Emotion (frequency) → Heart rhythm (pattern) → Neural signal (communication) → Hormone release (chemistry) → Physical state (experience).

Change the emotion, and the entire cascade reorganizes.

This is why practices like Reiki, meditation, and the Zone of Healing Genius Method™ work:
They don't just calm your mind — they *reprogram your chemistry.*

ENERGETIC INSIGHT

- Chaos is the body in survival; coherence is the body in creation.
- In chaos, you react; in coherence, you respond.
- In chaos, energy leaks; in coherence, energy regenerates.

The chemistry of coherence is your birthright — the natural alchemy of love, peace, and awareness flowing through the body.
It's the difference between living in reaction to life and *creating* life through resonance.

When you master this shift, your biology becomes your ally, your energy becomes your compass, and your emotions become your most reliable form of medicine.

"We built machines to analyze the world outside us, only to discover they mirror the intelligence within us."

Scientific Perspective — Dr. Valerie Hunt and the Edge of Chaos

Long before the term *coherence* became popular in energy medicine, UCLA physiologist **Dr. Valerie V. Hunt** was measuring it. Using electromyographic sensors and frequency-recording instruments in her laboratory, she discovered that the human energy field mirrors the chemistry of the nervous system. In her landmark work *Infinite Mind* (1996), Hunt described how healthy, creative states produce **coherent, information-rich wave patterns**, while stress and emotional suppression lead to **chaotic, disorganized vibrations** in both the muscles and the surrounding electromagnetic field.

Hunt referred to this threshold between order and disorder as *the edge of chaos*—a dynamic zone where the body's energy becomes unstable yet full of potential. When emotion and consciousness reintegrate, the chaotic field reorganizes into higher coherence, much like music resolving from dissonance into harmony.

Her findings support what both neuroscience and Reiki have long implied: the chemistry of peace and the frequency of coherence are inseparable. Whether measured as synchronized brain and heart rhythms or perceived as balanced energy flow, **coherence is the biological signature of harmony**, and **chaos is the signal of separation**. The key is not to fear chaos but to use it as a doorway; when energy reorganizes at a higher frequency, healing and evolution naturally follow.

WATER, EMOTION, AND THE RESONANCE OF INTENTION

Japanese researcher **Dr. Masaru Emoto** became internationally known for his pioneering—though often debated—experiments on the energetic properties of water. In his book *The Hidden Messages* *in Water*, Emoto photographed frozen water crystals after exposing the liquid to words, music, or focused intention. He found that water treated with expressions of love, gratitude, or harmonious sound formed **symmetrical, radiant crystals**, while water exposed to anger, fear, or discord produced **irregular, fragmented patterns**.

Although his methodology has faced criticism for lack of scientific control, the *metaphor* of his work remains profoundly relevant. Water, the element composing more than seventy percent of the human body, acts as a living conductor of vibration. Just as a single note can alter the resonance of a song, a single emotion can influence the structure of our inner waters.

From an energetic perspective, Emoto's findings mirror what both neuroscience and field research by Dr. Valerie Hunt have suggested: **emotion imprints frequency, and frequency shapes form.** When emotion is loving and coherent, molecular order increases; when it is chaotic or suppressed, molecular disorder follows. In this way, water becomes a mirror of consciousness—an ever-responsive medium reflecting the harmony or turbulence of the mind and heart.

Whether or not one accepts Emoto's photographs as empirical proof, they serve as a vivid illustration of the principle at the heart of this work:

Emotion is energy in motion, and its vibration organizes matter.

Our thoughts and feelings continuously ripple through the body's internal oceans. Each compassionate thought clarifies those waters; each unresolved fear clouds them. When coherence replaces chaos, the chemistry of the body reorganizes itself, much like frozen water returning to clear, crystalline beauty.

How Suppressed Emotions Distort Your Electromagnetic Field

When emotion is denied, energy is denied. The current that should move through you begins to stagnate—and the field around you starts to lose its harmony.

Every human being radiates an **electromagnetic field** — an energetic halo measurable by instruments such as magnetocardiograms and SQUID sensors.
Your heart generates the strongest of these fields, extending several feet around the body. Every beat transmits information about your emotional and physiological state, continuously interacting with your environment.

When emotion flows freely, that field is coherent: smooth, rhythmic, and radiant.
When emotion is **suppressed, avoided, or ignored**, the field becomes fragmented — like static in a signal or interference in music.
This disruption isn't symbolic; it's physical. Your emotional state directly alters the electromagnetic rhythms of your heart, brain, and nervous system.

WHAT SUPPRESSION DOES INSIDE THE BODY

When you swallow emotion — holding back tears, tightening your jaw, or "keeping it together" — your nervous system interprets the act as unresolved stress. The **vagus nerve** constricts, heart rate variability (HRV) declines, and the body shifts into sympathetic overdrive.
Energetically, that means less current moves through the meridians and chakras. The heart field loses its rhythm, and your inner communication network becomes distorted.

It's like crimping a hose — the pressure builds behind the blockage. The emotion doesn't disappear; it densifies. Over time, that energetic density can manifest as fatigue, tension, or chronic discomfort in the area where it's held.

THE RIPPLE EFFECT IN THE FIELD

Your electromagnetic field is a living record of your emotions. Suppressed feelings appear in that field as:

- **Distorted wave patterns:** abrupt spikes or dull, flattened regions.
- **Temperature fluctuations:** measurable changes in infrared imaging around areas of held emotion.
- **Weak coherence signals:** irregular HRV, inconsistent alpha rhythms, or diminished vitality perceived by sensitive practitioners.

Even your environment responds to these changes. People may feel uneasy near someone carrying intense unexpressed energy—not because of what's said, but because the field itself broadcasts the frequency of suppression.

RELEASING THE DISTORTION

Energy cannot be healed by denial; it must be **met, moved, and integrated.**
Here's a simple recalibration practice you can guide readers through:

1. **Acknowledge the emotion.**
   Whisper its name: *anger, grief, fear, shame.* Recognition starts the current flowing.
2. **Locate it in the body.**
   Is it heavy in your chest? Tight in your gut? Notice without judgment.

3. **Touch and breathe.**
   Place one hand where you feel it, the other over your heart.
   Inhale slowly through the nose, exhale through the mouth.
   Imagine energy moving between your hands in a gentle rhythm.
4. **Visualize coherence.**
   See the emotion's color or vibration softening and spreading evenly through the body.
5. **Reframe it.**
   Say: *"This energy is information returning to harmony."*

Within minutes, the electromagnetic field begins to stabilize. The heart rhythm smooths, brain waves align, and a sense of warmth or expansion replaces tension.

THE SCIENCE BEHIND THE SENSATION

The **HeartMath Institute** and other biofield researchers have shown that emotional states like appreciation and compassion generate smooth, sine-wave heart rhythms—an indicator of coherence. Conversely, frustration or suppression creates erratic heart-rate variability and irregular field patterns.
This proves that your emotional hygiene—how you feel and process energy—is as critical as your physical or mental health.

When you suppress emotion, you fragment your field.
When you express emotion consciously, you restore coherence.

ENERGETIC INSIGHT

Emotions are not meant to be stored; they're meant to be *streamed.*
Think of yourself as an instrument of frequency—your electromagnetic field the music you emit.
When emotion is acknowledged, your tone becomes clear and

resonant.

When emotion is repressed, the note wavers and falls out of tune.

By practicing awareness and release, you don't just regulate your nervous system—you *re-tune the symphony of your field.*
And in that resonance, healing isn't something you achieve; it becomes the natural song of your being.

"A coherent heart is the original supercomputer."

Practice: The 90-Second Energy Reset

Feel. Name. Breathe. Release.
One minute and a half is all it takes to change your chemistry,
recalibrate your frequency, and restore coherence.

Purpose

When an emotion rises—fear, frustration, sadness, or even overstimulation—you have about ninety seconds before your body's chemistry begins to shift.
If you consciously direct those ninety seconds, you transform reaction into release.

Each person experiences this differently. Some *hear* inner guidance, others *see* imagery, *feel* sensations, or simply *know* truth.
Choose the channel that feels most natural—or explore all four to activate your whole-brain, whole-body awareness.

Step 1 – Feel

Recognize that an emotional surge is energy asking to move.
Pause whatever you're doing, place both feet on the ground, and take one slow inhale through the nose.

Step 2 – Name

Whisper or think the emotion's name: *anger... sadness... fear... guilt... love... relief.*
Naming turns confusion into clarity. It signals your brain that you are conscious, safe, and present.

Step 3 – Breathe

Take three deep, coherent breaths.
Inhale for a count of five, exhale for a count of five.
With every exhale, imagine space opening inside you.

Step 4 – Release through Your Natural Channel

VISUAL – "See it clear."

- **Focus:** Third eye or forehead.
- **Process:** As you breathe, *see* the emotion as color or light swirling inside the body.
- Watch the color brighten or the light expand outward until it fills your entire aura.
- Say silently: *"I see clarity returning."*
- Notice the imagery change—dark to light, tight to spacious. That's energy transforming.

Visual Affirmation: "I see my energy realigning into harmony."

FEELER – "Feel it flow."

- **Focus:** Heart or solar plexus.
- **Process:** Place one hand where you sense the emotion. Feel the texture—warm, cool, tight, or fluttery.
- Keep breathing until the sensation begins to move, pulse, or soften.
- Whisper: *"It's safe to feel. I allow this energy to flow."*
- The release often feels like warmth, tingling, or tears—that's coherence returning.

Feeler Affirmation: "Every breath moves energy back into balance."

KNOWER – "Know it resets."

- **Focus:** Behind the sternum or crown of head.
- **Process:** Center your awareness and declare inwardly: *"I know this energy is information returning to harmony."*
- Trust that statement as absolute truth. Feel the shift that follows certainty—your system responds to conviction faster than analysis.
- Visualize a subtle "click" or alignment within you.

Knower Affirmation: "I know my field is reorganizing into coherence now."

AUDIO – "Hear it harmonize."

- **Focus:** Throat or heart area.
- **Process:** Exhale with sound—sigh, hum, or tone softly. Let the vibration resonate through your chest and throat.
- Imagine the sound smoothing jagged edges of emotion until only a calm hum remains.
- Say or hum words that comfort you: *"Peace... calm... release."*
- Sound entrains the body's frequency faster than thought.

Audio Affirmation: "My voice carries harmony through every cell."

Step 5 – Anchor the Shift

After about ninety seconds, you'll notice a subtle change—your breathing steadies, muscles loosen, and mind clears.
Touch your heart and say, *"I am coherent. I am clear."*

Stay still for a moment to memorize the sensation of balance.
Each time you practice, your nervous system learns to return to this state more quickly.

ENERGETIC INSIGHT

This 90-Second Reset is not suppression—it's transformation.
You're giving energy permission to complete its cycle.
Emotion becomes motion; motion becomes light; light becomes
coherence.

Use it any time you feel reactive, anxious, or disconnected.
In a minute and a half, you can change your entire field—and that's
how you begin living in your **Zone of Healing Genius.**

What You'll Feel Within 7 Days of Practicing Coherence

- Emotional clarity replacing overwhelm.
- Calmer sleep and clearer, more symbolic dreams.
- A natural lift in daily energy and mental focus.
- Easier communication and fewer reactive moments.
- Subtle intuitive nudges becoming stronger.
- Unexpected synchronicities — "chance" events aligning with
  purpose.

Keep note of these small wins. They're signs your nervous system
and biofield are re-harmonizing — proof that coherence isn't
imagined, it's embodied.

"AI can read your heartbeat, but only you can harmonize it."

MODERN EVIDENCE FOR ANCIENT WISDOM

For centuries, mystics and healers have spoken of light, frequency, and emotion as the true forces shaping health. Today, science is catching up.

We now live in a time when the world's most advanced technologies are validating what the ancients practiced intuitively — that **the human body is an electromagnetic system** responsive to thought, emotion, and environment.

The Science of Coherence

In 2022, the **HeartMath Institute's Global Coherence Initiative** recorded measurable synchrony between participants' heart rhythms and fluctuations in the Earth's magnetic field. When thousands entered states of compassion and gratitude simultaneously, global coherence data spiked — suggesting that human emotion literally influences planetary energy.

Meanwhile, neuroscientists studying brain–heart synchronization discovered that during meditative or loving states, the vagus nerve signals a cascade of hormones that calm inflammation, restore balance, and open perception. This biological coherence mirrors the energetic harmony described in Reiki, Qigong, and prayer traditions.

The Coherence Brain

Dr. **Joe Dispenza's EEG studies (2020–2024)** demonstrated that when individuals sustain elevated emotions, brain waves shift from chaotic beta to coherent alpha and gamma patterns — the same states associated with peak creativity, intuition, and spontaneous healing.

As participants held gratitude and love, measurable energy fields around the brain and heart expanded, recorded through advanced magnetoencephalography (MEG).

Bioelectromagnetism and the Future of Medicine

Research teams at **Stanford University** and **MIT Media Lab** (2021–2025) are exploring how the body's bioelectromagnetic field directs cellular communication. Experiments show that subtle electrical patterns precede tissue repair — echoing what energy healers have long sensed through the hands.
These studies are forming the foundation of a new medical frontier: *frequency-based diagnostics and regenerative therapies.*

Bridging Science and Spirit

When Dr. Valerie Hunt first recorded the human aura's electromagnetic frequencies, her instruments revealed what clairvoyants described for millennia.
When Dr. Masaru Emoto photographed water crystals transformed by thought and emotion, he proved that **vibration carries consciousness.**
Now, with AI and quantum sensors, we are seeing the same truth through data: that energy is intelligent, and consciousness is the field from which all form arises.

"Modern science is not replacing spirituality — it is translating it into a new language."

This is the bridge the **New Paradigm** stands upon: ancient intuition verified by modern evidence. The healer and the scientist are no longer opposites — they are now collaborators in decoding the light that animates life itself.

"Science Validating Spirit: 1920 → 2025"

Era	Discovery / Proof	Key Figures
1920s	Human electromagnetic field	Tesla, Georges Lakhovsky
1960s	Measurable aura frequencies	Dr. Valerie Hunt
1990s	Heart–brain coherence	HeartMath Institute
2000s	Consciousness & water memory	Dr. Masaru Emoto
2010s	Quantum biofield theory	Dr. Beverly Rubik
2020–2025	EEG, MEG, AI coherence mapping	Dispenza, Stanford, MIT

"The instruments of science can now detect what the heart has always known — that love is not an emotion, it's a measurable frequency."

3 | Heart-Brain Harmony

When the heart and brain synchronize, the entire body enters a state of intelligent rhythm. This is the true science of coherence.

Your heart does far more than pump blood. It is an **information center**, constantly sending electrical and electromagnetic signals to the brain and every cell of the body.
These signals influence emotional experience, perception, and even decision-making.

Modern research—particularly from the **HeartMath Institute**—has shown that the heart's rhythmic patterns are directly linked to emotional states. When you feel appreciation, love, or compassion, your heartbeat becomes smooth and orderly. When you feel fear, frustration, or anger, that rhythm turns erratic.

The quality of that rhythm—known as **heart rate variability (HRV)**—is one of the most accurate indicators of how well your body and mind are communicating.

THE SCIENCE OF COHERENCE

Coherence is the state in which the heart, brain, and nervous system operate in sync.
It's not just calmness—it's harmony in motion.
When coherence is high, electrical communication between the heart and brain flows freely, creating emotional stability, focus, and resilience.

In this state:

- The **vagus nerve** (the communication superhighway between heart and brain) sends balanced, rhythmic signals upward.
- The **brain** adjusts its chemistry, reducing stress hormones and increasing dopamine and serotonin.
- The **nervous system** enters equilibrium—neither overactive (fight or flight) nor underactive (freeze).
- The **electromagnetic field** of the heart radiates coherent frequencies that influence the brain waves of others nearby.

You literally become a transmitter of peace.

HEARTMATH DISCOVERIES

HeartMath's decades of biofeedback research have revealed that when a person experiences **positive emotions**, their heart rhythm forms smooth, repeating waves—like gentle ocean tides. Negative emotions produce chaotic, disordered patterns that scramble communication between the heart and brain.

High HRV (smooth variation between beats) equals adaptability, creativity, and health.
Low HRV (rigid, erratic rhythm) equals fatigue, confusion, and lowered immunity.

The heart leads, the brain follows, and the body obeys.

THE ROLE OF THE VAGUS NERVE

The **vagus nerve** is the body's coherence conductor.
It carries signals between the heart, lungs, gut, and brain—translating emotion into chemistry.
When the vagus tone is strong, your body shifts easily from stress to

relaxation.
When weak or overstimulated, you remain stuck in survival mode.

Every deep breath, every exhale of relief, strengthens vagal tone and raises coherence.
That's why practices like meditation, Reiki, chanting, and heart-focused breathing work: they **retrain the vagus nerve to choose peace.**

ENERGETIC VIEWPOINT

In energy medicine, this alignment is called **heart-brain resonance.**
When the heart (the seat of emotion) and the brain (the seat of perception) vibrate in the same rhythm, the entire chakra system stabilizes.
The electromagnetic field expands and brightens; intuition sharpens; the aura emits symmetry.

Science calls it *neurocardiac communication.*
Energy healing calls it *love.*

HEART–BRAIN COHERENCE PRACTICE

1. **Place one hand over your heart, the other over your abdomen.**
2. **Slow your breath.** Inhale for five counts, exhale for five. Imagine your breath moving through your heart—not your lungs.
3. **Recall a moment of genuine gratitude or compassion.** Feel it expand in your chest.
4. **Hold that feeling while continuing to breathe rhythmically.** Within 60–90 seconds, your HRV begins to smooth, and your brain synchronizes.

You'll know you've entered coherence when your body feels light, centered, and quietly joyful.
This is the **Zone of Healing Genius**—where physiology meets frequency.

- The brain processes thought; the heart processes truth.
- When they unite, intuition becomes intelligence.
- This is not mystical—it's measurable.
  The waveforms of heart and brain literally overlap when you are in love, gratitude, or creative flow.

When you live from this harmony, your biology becomes music.
You are no longer reacting to life—you are composing it.

Why Gratitude and Compassion Are the Highest Healing Frequencies

Gratitude and compassion are not emotions you feel — they are frequencies you become.

When your heart opens in gratitude or compassion, something extraordinary happens in both your **biology** and your **energy field.**
Your nervous system shifts from protection to connection.
Your chemistry changes from stress to regeneration.
And your electromagnetic field begins to broadcast harmony so coherent that it influences the space — and people — around you.

Gratitude and compassion are more than pleasant feelings; they are *vibrational signatures* that tell every cell in your body:

"I am safe. I am connected. I am home."

THE SCIENCE OF THE HEART'S HIGHEST FREQUENCIES

According to decades of research by the **HeartMath Institute**, feelings of appreciation and compassion produce the most stable and rhythmic heart rate patterns ever recorded.
This state — called **heart coherence** — generates smooth, sine-wave signals that synchronize brain function, balance hormone release, and enhance immune response.

In contrast, emotions like frustration or resentment create erratic heart rhythms that disrupt communication between the heart and brain.

Physiologically, gratitude and compassion:

- Increase **oxytocin**, the hormone of bonding and safety.
- Lower **cortisol** and **adrenaline**, reducing inflammation and aging.
- Raise **DHEA**, the hormone of vitality and regeneration.
- Strengthen **vagal tone**, improving emotional resilience and intuition.

Your heart's magnetic field — measurable up to several feet beyond your body — becomes more ordered and powerful.
The brain entrains to that rhythm, and your entire energy field becomes a transmitter of peace.

DR. VALERIE HUNT'S CONTRIBUTION: COHERENCE AS CONSCIOUSNESS

Dr. **Valerie Hunt**, whose laboratory work mapped the frequencies of the human biofield, observed that higher states of compassion and joy produced **organized, information-rich wave patterns** in both the body and its surrounding electromagnetic field.

In *Infinite Mind*, she described this coherence as "a frequency bridge between matter and consciousness."

In her recordings, moments of empathy and loving intention increased amplitude and smoothness in the human energy signal — measurable proof that positive emotion doesn't just *feel* different; it *vibrates* differently.

From Hunt's perspective, gratitude and compassion raise the human field into a higher bandwidth — one that transmits more data, intuition, and vitality.
In these moments, the body is not just healing; it's evolving.

MASARU EMOTO'S REFLECTION: WATER AS WITNESS

Dr. **Masaru Emoto's** water crystal photographs offer a visual metaphor for the same truth.
When water was exposed to words like *love* or *thank you*, the frozen crystals formed symmetrical, radiant patterns.
When subjected to anger or hatred, the formations collapsed into chaos.

Since the human body is mostly water, these images remind us that our inner waters are constantly responding to emotional frequency. A mind steeped in gratitude creates order within its own molecular landscape; a heart steeped in compassion restores flow where energy once stagnated.

SHIFT YOUR STATE, SHIFT YOUR FREQUENCY

Many transformational teachers point to the same practical truth: change your state, and you change your life. Leading voices in personal performance emphasize that the body's physiology and the mind's story are inseparable — shift the body and the nervous system, and the mind follows. This is precisely what energy medicine calls coherence: an aligned heart–brain rhythm that interrupts old reactive loops and creates space for new patterns. Practitioners such as Tony Robbins have long taught techniques for changing physical state (breath, posture, focused sensation) as the fastest way to break old patterns.

ENERGETIC INSIGHT

From the energetic viewpoint, gratitude and compassion are **unifying currents**.
They dissolve resistance, bridge polarity, and expand the auric field.
Where lower emotions contract and isolate, these higher frequencies expand and integrate.
They are the "neutralizing harmonics" — capable of transmuting chaos into coherence.

In Reiki, when practitioners hold gratitude for the energy itself, the flow amplifies.
In meditation, when compassion arises naturally, the field brightens.
Both frequencies open the heart chakra fully, allowing the soul's light to circulate through every layer of being.

"AI will decode the signals of the body, but only consciousness can interpret the language of the soul."

PRACTICE – THE COHERENCE OF GRATITUDE AND COMPASSION

1. **Breathe into the Heart:**
    Inhale slowly through your nose for five counts, exhale for five.
    Imagine your breath flowing in and out of your heart.
2. **Recall a Moment of Genuine Gratitude:**
    It could be as simple as sunlight on your face, laughter with a friend, or the gift of breath itself.
    Let that feeling expand until it fills your chest.
3. **Extend Compassion:**
    Picture someone — even yourself — who could use kindness.
    Send them the energy of peace through your breath.
4. **Sense the Field:**
    Notice warmth in your chest, a subtle hum, or light around your body.
    That is your electromagnetic field reorganizing into coherence.

Within ninety seconds, your heart rhythm smooths, your brain waves balance, and your chemistry shifts toward healing.

THE RIPPLE EFFECT

Gratitude and compassion don't stop at your skin.
Studies using magnetometers have shown that a coherent heart field can influence others nearby, helping synchronize their rhythms too.
Your peace becomes contagious.
Your field becomes medicine.

When you live in gratitude, you emit coherence.
When you live in compassion, you transmit healing.

This is why these two emotions are the **highest healing frequencies**: they transform the individual — and through resonance — they begin to heal the collective.

"In the medicine of the future, coherence will be the new vital sign."

How Thought Follows Rhythm — Aligning the Two Creates Genius

Genius is not a gift reserved for a few — it's a frequency available to anyone whose thoughts move in rhythm with their inner energy.

When your thoughts are scattered, looping, or fearful, your brainwaves become fragmented.
When your emotions are erratic or suppressed, your heart rhythm becomes jagged.
But when your **heart rhythm** and **thought rhythm** align — when the pulse of feeling and the pattern of thinking move in the same tempo — something remarkable happens.
Your entire system enters a state of flow.
This is the frequency of genius.

THE SCIENCE OF RHYTHMIC INTELLIGENCE

Every thought you have is accompanied by an electrical wave.
Every heartbeat generates a magnetic field.
When the rhythm of the heart entrains the rhythm of the brain, **communication between the two becomes seamless** — thought becomes clear, intuitive, and creative rather than repetitive or defensive.

Neuroscience shows that the brain oscillates in rhythmic patterns — alpha, beta, theta, gamma — each corresponding to a state of consciousness.

- **Beta** is active thinking, problem-solving.
- **Alpha** is creative flow and visualization.
- **Theta** is intuitive insight and memory integration.
- **Gamma** is higher awareness and integration — the "aha!" frequency.

The heart's coherent rhythm can *entrain* these brainwaves upward — lifting them from survival (beta) into creativity (alpha/theta) and integration (gamma).
This is not metaphoric; EEG and HRV coherence research show the two systems lock into phase when emotion and attention align.

In that synchronization, thought stops being reaction — it becomes revelation.

THE RHYTHM OF THE HEART AS THE METRONOME OF THOUGHT

Your heart is your body's metronome — the keeper of biological time.
Every beat sends signals through the vagus nerve to regulate your brain's rhythmic patterns.
When you are stressed or disconnected, that rhythm becomes irregular; thought fragments, memory weakens, and creativity collapses.

But when you breathe with rhythm and fill that rhythm with gratitude or compassion, your heartbeat stabilizes — and your brain falls into sync.
That's when insight flows effortlessly.
You're not thinking *harder*; you're thinking *in tune*.

This is the difference between forcing intelligence and allowing genius.

ENERGETIC VIEWPOINT — THE PULSE OF CREATION

From an energy perspective, rhythm is the **bridge between matter and consciousness.**
Dr. Valerie Hunt's measurements of the human field showed that

coherent rhythms in the body's electromagnetic waves corresponded with **higher states of awareness** and **expanded intuition** — what she called "the bandwidth of higher consciousness."

When rhythm is disturbed, the field collapses into chaos; when rhythm is restored, energy reorganizes into creative intelligence.

This is why all ancient healing and spiritual traditions use rhythm — drumming, chanting, breathwork, mantra, walking meditation.
Rhythm grounds frequency into form.
It teaches the body and soul to move as one.

MASARU EMOTO'S REFLECTION — THOUGHT SHAPES FORM THROUGH RHYTHM

Dr. Masaru Emoto's water crystal images also demonstrate this principle in visual form.
Water exposed to music with steady, harmonious rhythm — classical, sacred chant, or gentle melody — produced stunningly symmetrical crystals.
Water exposed to irregular, chaotic noise created distorted, fragmented shapes.
Our thoughts, like that music, ripple through our body's inner waters.

When your thinking holds rhythm — measured by calm breath and coherent heart rate — your internal water harmonizes.
When your thoughts scatter or race, your inner waters lose structure.

Rhythm, then, is the conductor of thought's creative power.

THE GENIUS FREQUENCY

"Genius" is not a trait of IQ — it is a **frequency of alignment.**
It emerges when three rhythms synchronize:

1. The **heart rhythm** (emotion and intuition)
2. The **brain rhythm** (thought and logic)
3. The **breath rhythm** (life force and presence)

When these three move together, energy flows without resistance.
You access higher insight not by trying, but by attuning.

Coherence = Rhythm = Genius.

This is the foundation of what I call *The Zone of Healing Genius* —
the point where thought no longer drives energy, but energy drives
thought.

PRACTICE – ALIGNING THOUGHT AND RHYTHM

1. **Sit quietly** and place one hand on your heart.
2. **Breathe in rhythm:** five seconds in, five seconds out.
3. **Notice your thoughts.** Don't chase them — feel their tempo.
   Are they rushing, looping, hesitant?
4. **Gently match your breath to your thoughts.** Slow your
   breathing until your thoughts begin to slow, too.
5. **Add gratitude.** Feel appreciation for something simple —
   your breath, your heartbeat, the moment itself.
6. **Listen inwardly.** At some point, you'll feel the thoughts
   begin to follow the rhythm of your heart.

That's the moment of alignment — when inspiration, intuition, and
clarity fuse.
In that space, answers appear effortlessly.

ENERGETIC INSIGHT

You don't think your way into genius.
You *breathe* your way into it.
When the rhythm of your thought matches the rhythm of your heart, you awaken what Tesla, Einstein, and every mystic called the **field of pure intelligence** — the creative current that connects all life.

And once you touch that rhythm, you'll never again doubt your inner genius — because you'll *feel* it moving through you.

*"Healing will no longer mean fighting disease
— it will mean restoring rhythm."*

The 3 Frequencies of Genius: Emotional, Mental, and Spiritual Alignment

Genius is not a thought — it's a resonance.
When your emotional, mental, and spiritual frequencies vibrate in harmony, you awaken the consciousness that creates worlds.

1. THE EMOTIONAL FREQUENCY — THE HEART'S CURRENT

The emotional body is your energy's *engine*.
It moves faster than thought and carries the charge that tells the universe what frequency you're operating on.
When emotion is coherent (calm, grateful, compassionate), your **heart rhythm stabilizes** and your field expands.
When emotion is chaotic (fear, resentment, shame), your heart rhythm collapses, and your body's intelligence fragments.

Emotion is not a weakness — it's your navigation system.
When the heart's current is balanced, you can *feel truth* instantly.
Your body becomes a compass of coherence, pulling your thoughts and actions into alignment.

Energetic mantra:

"My emotions are energy in motion — I choose their direction."

2. THE MENTAL FREQUENCY — THE MIND'S WAVE

The mental body translates energy into form.
It turns vibration into ideas, words, and images.
But if the mind spins in survival mode, it loses its ability to receive higher frequencies.

When emotion and breath are chaotic, brainwaves become jagged
— like static interrupting a broadcast.
When emotion softens and rhythm steadies, the brain synchronizes
into **alpha and theta waves** — the creative frequencies where
innovation and intuition arise.

This is what we call *the genius wave*: the state where the left and
right hemispheres of the brain communicate fluidly, logic and
imagination dance together, and insight flows without resistance.

Energetic mantra:

"My thoughts follow rhythm; my mind follows peace."

3. THE SPIRITUAL FREQUENCY — THE SOUL'S LIGHT

The spiritual body is your **field of coherence** — the luminous
frequency that connects you to Source intelligence.
It is not bound by time, belief, or biology.
When emotional energy flows and the mind is rhythmic, the soul's
light can inhabit the body fully.
This is the moment of embodiment — the merging of spirit and
form.

Here, intuition becomes instantaneous knowing.
Healing becomes natural.
You stop chasing guidance and start *being* it.

This is the **Zone of Healing Genius** — where the divine intelligence
that animates all life moves through you as clear perception,
compassion, and creativity.

Energetic mantra:

"When my soul's light aligns with my heart and mind, I become the instrument of creation."

INTEGRATION INSIGHT

You are an orchestra of frequencies:

- The **heart** sets the emotional rhythm,
- The **mind** translates it into thought,
- The **soul** amplifies it into purpose.

When one instrument is out of tune, life feels discordant.
But when all three align, the music of genius plays through you —
effortlessly, authentically, and continuously.

The greatest form of healing is harmony.
The greatest form of intelligence is coherence.

"The doctors of tomorrow will speak the languages of energy, data, and love."

Practice: The 3-Minute Coherence Breath

Breathe as though your heart and brain are one instrument — each breath a note that restores harmony.

Purpose

The **3-Minute Coherence Breath** is a rapid recalibration technique that unites your emotional, mental, and spiritual frequencies.
It's simple, measurable, and profound.
In just three minutes, you can shift from mental chaos to calm clarity, synchronize your heart and brain, and activate what science calls *neurocardiac coherence* — and what I call *The Zone of Healing Genius.*

You're not forcing the body to relax; you're inviting energy to realign. You'll know it's working when your breathing slows naturally, your thoughts quiet, and a warm or luminous feeling begins to radiate from your chest.

Step 1: Prepare — The Posture of Presence

Sit or stand comfortably with both feet grounded.
Straighten your spine just enough to let energy move freely.
Place one hand on your **heart** and one on your **abdomen** — this connects breath (life force) with emotion (heart rhythm).

Close your eyes.
Inhale slowly through your nose for **five counts**, exhale through your mouth for **five counts**.
Do not force the breath — let it flow like an ocean tide.

Step 2: Focus — Enter the Heart

Shift your awareness from the mind into the space beneath your hand on your heart.
Imagine your breath flowing in and out through your heart center.
As you do, feel the energy between your hands begin to synchronize — the abdomen following the heart's rhythm.

Whisper silently or aloud:

"I am breathing coherence."

Within seconds, your nervous system begins to balance, your vagus nerve relaxes, and your electromagnetic field expands.

Step 3: Feel — Awaken Gratitude

Now, call to mind a moment of pure gratitude or compassion — something that makes your heart swell effortlessly.
It could be a memory, a person, a pet, a sunrise, or simply the feeling of breath itself.

Feel it grow until it fills your chest like warm light.
This emotion is the frequency carrier — it tells your body *you are safe to open.*

Step 4: Align — Engage Your Natural Channel

Each person experiences coherence differently. Use the sensory pathway that feels most natural to you — or explore them all:

Visual Channel – "See the Rhythm"

Imagine waves of soft golden light expanding from your heart, pulsing outward in perfect symmetry.

Each breath paints light through your aura — steady, luminous, coherent.
Say inwardly: *"I see my energy glowing in perfect balance."*

Feeler Channel – "Feel the Flow"

Sense the movement of energy through your body — a warmth spreading from your chest, a gentle tingling in your hands or spine. Allow any tension to melt.
Say: *"I feel the rhythm of life within me."*

Knower Channel – "Know the Alignment"

Focus on the certainty that your body knows how to heal and your energy knows where to flow.
You don't have to understand the process — just know that coherence is happening.
Say: *"I know my system is harmonizing with divine intelligence."*

Audio Channel – "Hear the Harmony"

Listen for the subtle hum of your breath, the faint beat of your heart, or even an imagined tone of peace.
Let the sound stabilize your frequency.
Whisper: *"I hear the song of coherence within me."*

Step 5: Integrate — Anchor the Shift

Continue breathing rhythmically for three full minutes.
If your mind wanders, simply return to your heart's rhythm.
By the third minute, your heart and brain are synchronized, your chemistry recalibrated, and your field expanded.

To complete, inhale deeply and hold for a moment, then exhale with the words:

"I am aligned — body, mind, and soul."

Stay in the silence that follows — that stillness *is* coherence.

ENERGETIC INSIGHT

This breath aligns all three frequencies of genius:

- **Emotion** (heart rhythm) creates magnetic coherence.
- **Thought** (brain rhythm) follows and organizes around it.
- **Spirit** (light frequency) amplifies and integrates them both.

With practice, the **3-Minute Coherence Breath** becomes your reset button — a way to return to your natural state of harmony anytime, anywhere.

Use it before meditation, healing sessions, creative work, or any time you feel disoriented or disconnected.
It doesn't just calm you — it *reprograms* your frequency to match genius.

One breath, one rhythm, one alignment — that's how healing becomes creation.

"The next frontier of medicine isn't mechanical — it's vibrational."

The Genius Field: How Coherence Expands Intuition, Creativity, and Healing

When the heart and brain synchronize, they generate a field of order so powerful that it reorganizes not just the body, but reality itself.

WHAT IS THE GENIUS FIELD?

The *Genius Field* is not a place — it's a **frequency of coherence**.
It's the electromagnetic harmony produced when your emotional, mental, and spiritual energies vibrate in alignment.
You feel it as flow, inspiration, ease, and deep intuitive knowing.

Science calls it *heart–brain coherence.*
Mystics call it *the field of consciousness.*
I call it **the Zone of Healing Genius.**

When you maintain coherence long enough, your energy field expands, your perception heightens, and you begin to access information that exists *beyond the limits of ordinary awareness.*

NEUROSCIENCE MEETS ENERGY MEDICINE

In states of coherence, the brain shifts from survival-driven beta activity into **alpha and gamma rhythms** — the brainwaves of creativity, empathy, and insight.
Functional MRI studies show that the prefrontal cortex (intuition and decision-making) lights up while the amygdala (fear center) quiets down.
You literally *open the neural gates of genius.*

At the same time, the heart's magnetic field — measurable several feet beyond the body — becomes smooth and powerful, transmitting coherent frequencies that affect both your cells and your surroundings.

In Reiki terms, this is *expanded auric resonance*; in physics, it's constructive interference.

Either way, the energy field amplifies.

When heart and brain share one rhythm, thought turns into creation.

THE THREE EXPANSIONS OF THE GENIUS FIELD

1. Intuition – The Language of the Field

Coherence sharpens intuitive perception.

Signals that were once drowned out by emotional noise become clear and immediate.

You begin to "know" things before the mind reasons them out — a phenomenon Valerie Hunt observed as **increased frequency amplitude** in the upper electromagnetic ranges of the human field during intuitive insight.

This isn't supernatural; it's super-sensitive.

Your body is a tuned receiver — and coherence improves the signal.

2. Creativity – The Flow of Innovation

In the Genius Field, ideas arrive fully formed, as if dropped into awareness.

This is the "flow state" described by artists, inventors, and healers alike.

Neuro-cardiac synchronization allows the hemispheres of the brain to communicate fluently, merging logic and imagination into a single current.

Dr. Masaru Emoto's water imagery offers a metaphor here: harmonious vibration creates beauty and structure.

When your thoughts, emotions, and energy vibrate coherently, the *water within you* arranges itself into order — and new creations take form effortlessly.

3. Healing – The Restoration of Resonance

Healing is not the removal of disease; it is the **return of resonance.**
In coherence, the immune, endocrine, and nervous systems operate as one symphony.
Cells communicate faster, inflammation decreases, and DNA repair genes activate.
Energetically, the field becomes self-correcting — distortions smooth, flow returns, and the body remembers its original blueprint of wholeness.

The more time you spend in coherence, the more your field entrains others toward it.
This is why a calm healer can regulate a chaotic client's energy simply by presence.
It is resonance physics — the higher frequency reorganizes the lower.

HOW TO ACCESS THE GENIUS FIELD

You enter the Genius Field through rhythm, emotion, and intention — not through force.

1. **Breathe rhythmically** until the heart leads the mind.
2. **Feel gratitude or compassion** until emotion steadies into coherence.
3. **Hold intention lightly** — not as demand, but as vibration.

Stay in that harmony, and ideas, guidance, and healing flow through you as naturally as breath.

ENERGETIC INSIGHT

Every person carries the blueprint of genius — not as a talent, but as a *frequency pattern.*
When coherence becomes your baseline, you think faster but with ease, feel deeper but with peace, and heal not by effort but by resonance.

The Genius Field is the next evolution of healing — where biology meets frequency, and human consciousness remembers its creative power.

"Healing will no longer mean fighting disease — it will mean restoring rhythm."

Genius Field Activation — A 2-Minute Alignment Practice

Close your eyes and breathe... You're about to remember what it feels like to be whole, luminous, and infinitely intelligent.

Purpose

This practice activates the three frequencies of genius — **emotional, mental, and spiritual alignment** — through breath, focus, and intention.
It teaches your body to recall coherence as its natural state and your energy field to broadcast genius frequency effortlessly.

Step 1 – Connect to the Breath (10 seconds)

Inhale slowly through your nose for a count of **five**.
Exhale gently through your mouth for **five**.
Imagine the breath flowing *in and out through your heart.*
Each breath synchronizes your body's rhythm with the rhythm of the universe.

Whisper inwardly:

"I breathe coherence."

Step 2 – Activate the Heart (30 seconds)

Place one hand on your chest.
Think of a moment of deep **gratitude or compassion** — something that instantly warms you from the inside.
Let that emotion expand through your heart like light radiating in every direction.

Feel it moving beyond your skin, surrounding you in a soft, pulsing glow.

Your heart is now broadcasting the frequency of harmony.

Step 3 – Align the Mind (30 seconds)

Bring your awareness to your forehead — the space of insight.
Imagine your thoughts slowing, rearranging into waves that match your heartbeat.
You are no longer thinking; you are *receiving.*
See or sense a gentle current of golden light linking your heart and mind — flowing back and forth in perfect rhythm.

Whisper inwardly:

"My thoughts follow the rhythm of my heart."

Step 4 – Awaken the Field (40 seconds)

Now imagine that rhythm expanding outward —
your entire aura glowing, humming, resonating with coherent light.
You may see colors, feel warmth, or simply *know* that you are connected to something vast and intelligent.

Allow that light to touch every cell, every thought, every possibility.
This is the **Genius Field** — the living network of consciousness that carries information, healing, and creation.

Breathe into it.
Trust it.
Let it remember you.

Step 5 – Anchor the Frequency (10 seconds)

Bring both hands to your heart and whisper:

"I am coherent. I am creative. I am connected."

Inhale once more and exhale slowly.
Open your eyes.

ENERGETIC INSIGHT

Every time you activate this state — even for two minutes — your electromagnetic field reorganizes.
Heart and brain move into resonance, the mind quiets, and intuition awakens.
You become a living transmitter of the Genius Field itself.

This is not visualization. This is vibration.
This is your Zone of Healing Genius.

"AI will predict illness, but consciousness will prevent it."

REFLECTION: LIVING FROM THE GENIUS FIELD

Genius is not found — it's felt. It lives in the stillness that follows coherence.

Take a moment after completing the *Genius Field Activation* to capture what moved through you.
Your first impressions are the purest — they come from the heart, not the analytical mind.

Step 1 – Record the Sensation

Ask yourself:

- What did I feel in my body when I entered coherence? *(Warmth, vibration, peace, expansion, tingling, lightness?)*
- Did I notice a shift in breath, heartbeat, or tension?
- Where in my body did I sense energy flowing most strongly?

Write without editing. Sensations are language — your body's way of showing that alignment is real.

Step 2 – Observe the Mind

Now notice what changed in your thoughts.

- Did the mind quiet or focus?
- Did a solution, memory, or intuitive idea arise spontaneously?
- If your thoughts carried color, rhythm, or sound — what would they be?

Record them. These are glimpses of your *Genius Frequency* — how creativity speaks through you.

Step 3 – Feel the Field

Close your eyes briefly and sense the space around your body.
Does it feel lighter, wider, softer, or more radiant than before?
That's your electromagnetic field expanding.

Note any colors, images, or subtle impressions.
Even a single word that captures the feeling — *peace, power, light, trust* — becomes an anchor you can return to later.

Step 4 – Anchor the Memory

On the last line of your journal page, write this statement:

*"This is what coherence feels like for me.
This is the frequency of my Genius Field."*

Read it aloud.
The voice imprints the vibration into your nervous system, strengthening the neural and energetic pathways that support this state.

The more often you reflect immediately after entering coherence, the faster your body remembers how to return.
Journaling crystallizes vibration into form — it bridges energy into expression.

Each reflection is a breadcrumb leading you back to your Genius Field.
Follow it daily until coherence becomes your way of being.

4 | State → Story → Stractegy

Energy creates emotion. Emotion creates meaning. Meaning creates motion.

When you master these three, you don't just heal — you *re-write reality*.

STATE | YOUR VIBRATIONAL FREQUENCY IN THE MOMENT

Your **state** is the real-time frequency your field is broadcasting.
It's the combination of your chemistry, breath, posture, and focus — the electromagnetic tone of your being.

Every thought, every feeling, every movement sends a signal.
That signal tells your nervous system how to behave, your cells how to respond, and even your environment how to mirror you.

When your state vibrates at fear, frustration, or depletion, coherence collapses and the world reflects disorder.
When your state vibrates at calm confidence or gratitude, the field organizes itself around balance and opportunity.

In this book's language:

State = Frequency.
You cannot think your way out of a low frequency; you must *feel* and *breathe* your way into a higher one.

Practice prompt:
Pause three times a day and ask, *"What frequency am I living from right now?"*
Then shift with one breath, one posture, one intention.

STORY | THE MEANING YOUR FREQUENCY CREATES

Your **story** is the narrative your mind builds to justify your frequency.
It's the explanation your brain invents for why you feel the way you do.
If your frequency is low, your story will sound like limitation; if your frequency is high, the story expands into possibility.

Energy moves first; meaning follows.
That's why changing your emotional frequency often rewrites your mental script automatically.

In energy medicine, the stories we tell become *vibrational programs* in the field — loops that replay until we interrupt them with a new signal.
Healing requires more than affirmations; it requires *resonance with a different story.*

Re-framing tool:
When you catch yourself in an old loop ("I always get sick," "I never have time," "People drain me"), place your hand on your heart and say:

"That story was created from a lower frequency.
I now choose the vibration of harmony."

Your body feels truth before your mind believes it.

STRATEGY | THE RITUALS THAT SUSTAIN COHERENCE

Strategy is not a plan — it's a *practice.*
It's what keeps your field stable when life tests your alignment.

Breath, gratitude, movement, touch, hydration, prayer, sound, and nature — these are the tools that regulate frequency.
Used consistently, they teach your nervous system that coherence is the default, not the exception.

A strategy rooted in energy follows three principles:

1. **Consistency over intensity.**
   Small, rhythmic acts (3-Minute Coherence Breath, morning gratitude, evening release) build energetic muscle faster than occasional intensity.
2. **Embodiment over analysis.**
   Don't think your rituals — *feel* them.
   Coherence is experienced through sensation, not theory.
3. **Integration over isolation.**
   Align rituals with daily life — breathe while driving, ground while cooking, listen inward while walking.
   Every moment becomes practice.

Strategy = Sustainability.
Without ritual, frequency fades. With ritual, coherence becomes identity.

REFLECTION | REWRITING THE HEALING STORY

Old energetic loops — the *Healer's Wound, Over-Thinker, Not-Enough, Hidden Anger,* or *Fear of Visibility* — are just stories recorded in vibration.
Each time you enter coherence, you weaken their signal.

Reflection Exercise:

1. Identify one repeating story that limits your energy.
2. Ask: *"What frequency created this?"*
3. Use the **90-Second Energy Reset** to release the emotion behind it.
4. Replace the vibration with gratitude, compassion, or joy.
5. Record the new story in your journal as if it has already happened.

This isn't imagination — it's energetic re-coding.
You are reprogramming your biofield to broadcast a new narrative.

ENERGETIC INSIGHT

- **State** determines the frequency you transmit.
- **Story** translates that frequency into meaning.
- **Strategy** anchors the vibration into daily reality.

When all three align, you live in what Tony Robbins calls "peak state" and what this book calls **The Zone of Healing Genius** — a place where thought, emotion, and action vibrate in unison with your highest coherence.

In that rhythm, healing is no longer recovery — it's creation.

Pause and Remember

If you're reading this and feeling the stir of old emotions — that's not regression, it's release.
Healing is not a straight line; it's a spiral returning you to the places that need love, not judgment.
Pause. Place your hand over your heart.
Breathe.
You are not behind; you are becoming whole.
Every moment you choose coherence, you're teaching your body what safety feels like again.

Reader Journal Reflection

What does coherence feel like for me today?

Write freely. Describe sensations, colors, images, or memories that arise when you feel harmony.
Let the page reflect what words cannot yet express.

"When technology evolves without consciousness, it divides. When consciousness evolves through technology, it unites."

PART II – THE ENERGETIC REPROGRAMMING METHOD

Transformation happens when awareness becomes embodied.

You can understand energy. You can even feel it.
But true transformation only occurs when awareness moves beyond
thought and takes residence in the body — when knowledge
becomes *experience*.

This is where your healing becomes your genius.
In this section, we move from theory to embodiment — from
knowing about coherence to living it.
The *Energetic Reprogramming Method* is designed to recalibrate
every level of your being — emotional, mental, physical, and spiritual
— into one synchronized intelligence.

"Our creations — from machines to medicine
— are only as coherent as their creators."

5 | Mapping the Four Bodies of Intelligence

You are not a mind trying to heal a body — you are four dimensions of intelligence remembering how to move as one.

THE FOUR BODIES OF INTELLIGENCE

In energy medicine, a human being is a multidimensional system composed of four interrelated layers — each carrying its own frequency, language, and wisdom.

These are:

1. **The Emotional Body** — the energy of feeling.
2. **The Mental Body** — the energy of thought.
3. **The Physical Body** — the energy of form.
4. **The Spiritual Body** — the energy of consciousness.

Each body has its own intelligence, but no single one operates independently.
When they communicate clearly, you live in harmony; when they disconnect, you experience dis-ease — whether that shows up as anxiety, fatigue, or physical pain.

Healing, therefore, is not fixing what's broken; it's restoring communication across all four bodies so that life-force can flow freely.

1. THE EMOTIONAL BODY — THE LANGUAGE OF FREQUENCY

The Emotional Body is your **energetic messenger.**
It translates vibration into feeling — joy, sadness, anger, love, grief, peace.
When you ignore emotion, energy stagnates; when you honor it, energy moves.

Emotion is the **first responder** in your system. It feels truth before the mind interprets it.
That's why intuition speaks through sensation — chills, warmth, tears, tightness.
These aren't reactions to life; they're communication from your energy field.

To reprogram at this level, you must *feel to heal.*
Emotion, once allowed, becomes energy in motion again — returning you to coherence.

Mantra: "My emotions are the voice of my energy field."

2. THE MENTAL BODY — THE ARCHITECT OF MEANING

The Mental Body organizes emotion into understanding.
It's your inner storyteller — the part that assigns meaning to everything you feel and experience.

When this body is balanced, thought is clear, creative, and solution-oriented.
When out of sync, it becomes analytical, looping, or fearful.

The mind is powerful, but it can't heal through logic alone — it must partner with emotion.

In the Energetic Reprogramming Method, we don't silence thought; we **train it to follow rhythm** — aligning the mental current with the emotional frequency and physical breath.

This is where self-sabotage ends, because the mind finally stops fighting the heart.

Mantra: "My thoughts align with the rhythm of truth."

3. THE PHYSICAL BODY — THE INSTRUMENT OF INTEGRATION

The Physical Body is where energy becomes matter — your lived experience.
It stores every frequency the others create.
Tension, illness, or fatigue are not enemies; they are *embodied communication* from your other layers.

When energy stagnates in the emotional or mental field, the body absorbs the signal as density — muscles tighten, organs weaken, hormones misfire.
When coherence returns, the same energy releases as warmth, movement, or lightness.

Your body is the living map of your consciousness.
By working through touch, breath, and motion, you can reprogram stored frequencies and teach the body that safety is its natural state again.

Mantra: "My body is the physical expression of my energy in balance."

4. THE SPIRITUAL BODY — THE FIELD OF INFINITE INTELLIGENCE

The Spiritual Body is your highest frequency — the field of light and information that connects you to Source.
It doesn't operate through emotion or thought, but through *knowing.*
It is your intuition, your inner healer, your timeless awareness.

When disconnected from the lower three bodies, the spiritual body can feel distant or unreachable — as if wisdom exists "out there."
But when integrated, it flows through every cell as clarity, peace, and purpose.

Dr. Valerie Hunt described this as the *higher bandwidth* of human energy — the moment when the body's electromagnetic frequencies become so coherent that they access transpersonal awareness.
This is not escape from the body — it is the full embodiment of light within it.

Mantra: "My spirit animates every part of me with divine intelligence."

INTEGRATION: THE FOUR BODIES AS ONE SYSTEM

Imagine these four bodies as concentric spheres of energy, all sharing one vibration:

- The **Physical** is the vessel.
- The **Emotional** is the current.
- The **Mental** is the pattern.
- The **Spiritual** is the light animating them all.

When coherence flows through all four, your system becomes a unified field of intelligence — what I call **Embodied Awareness.**

From this state, healing, creativity, and intuition are not separate skills; they are *side effects* of alignment.

PRACTICE – THE 4-BODY SCAN

1. **Breathe slowly** and bring your awareness into your body.
2. **Emotional Body:** Ask, "What am I feeling right now?" Let the emotion move like water.
3. **Mental Body:** Ask, "What story am I telling about this feeling?"
4. **Physical Body:** Place a hand wherever you sense tension. Breathe love into that space.
5. **Spiritual Body:** Ask, "What truth is this moment trying to reveal?"

Feel all four layers begin to hum together — one resonance, one intelligence.

Finish by saying:

"All parts of me are listening. All parts of me are aligned."

ENERGETIC INSIGHT

You are not four separate beings trying to get along.
You are one consciousness expressing through four frequencies of intelligence.
When these harmonize, awareness becomes embodied — and embodiment becomes transformation.

The healer, the healed, and the healing are not three things.
They are one vibration, remembered through coherence.

How Imbalance in One Distorts All

You are a symphony of four instruments — emotional, mental, physical, and spiritual. When even one plays out of tune, the entire harmony shifts.

THE INTERCONNECTED DESIGN OF THE FOUR BODIES

Each body of intelligence — emotional, mental, physical, and spiritual — is a current in the same electrical circuit.
They don't operate in isolation; they *mirror and magnify* one another.
When one frequency weakens or becomes distorted, it sends feedback through the entire system.

Think of it like tuning forks — when one vibrates irregularly, the others begin to resonate with that distortion.
This is how subtle imbalance becomes chronic pattern, and chronic pattern becomes illness, disconnection, or confusion.

Healing, therefore, is not about fixing a symptom; it's about restoring **resonance across the network.**

WHEN THE EMOTIONAL BODY IS IMBALANCED

The emotional field governs vibration — it is your first responder to life.
When emotion is repressed, denied, or overly amplified, the current becomes chaotic.
That chaos sends erratic signals through the vagus nerve and hormonal system, affecting the physical body's chemistry and the mind's clarity.

- **Signs:** Mood swings, anxiety, impulsivity, emotional numbness, inner heaviness.
- **How It Affects the Others:**
  - *Mental Body:* Thought loops amplify drama or fear.
  - *Physical Body:* Adrenal stress, digestive tension, fatigue.
  - *Spiritual Body:* Diminished sense of connection or purpose.

An unexpressed emotion doesn't disappear; it changes form.

Until it moves, the entire field vibrates in disharmony.
Releasing emotion through awareness, breath, or energy work instantly rebalances the circuit.

WHEN THE MENTAL BODY IS IMBALANCED

The mental field shapes meaning — it decides what emotion *means*.
When the mind becomes overactive, rigid, or self-critical, it dominates the field and drowns out intuition.
The heart's rhythm falters because the brain keeps sending signals of threat or inadequacy.

- **Signs:** Overthinking, perfectionism, confusion, insomnia, feeling "stuck in your head."
- **How It Affects the Others:**
  - *Emotional Body:* Suppression or intensification of feeling.
  - *Physical Body:* Head tension, jaw clenching, nervous exhaustion.
  - *Spiritual Body:* Disconnection from flow and synchronicity.

When the mind stops listening to the heart, coherence collapses.

Balance returns when thought follows rhythm — when the mind remembers its role is to serve, not steer, the energy.

WHEN THE PHYSICAL BODY IS IMBALANCED

The physical layer is the anchor of the other three — it grounds energy into tangible experience.
When the body is neglected, overdriven, or ignored, the feedback to the higher layers weakens.
Without grounding, intuition becomes scattered and emotions overtake clarity.

- **Signs:** Chronic fatigue, muscle tension, pain, digestive issues, burnout.
- **How It Affects the Others:**
    - *Emotional Body:* Irritability, low resilience.
    - *Mental Body:* Fog, lack of motivation.
    - *Spiritual Body:* Feeling "cut off" or unworthy.

The body is not the problem — it's the messenger.

When you move, hydrate, rest, and breathe, you're not just caring for tissue — you're restoring the physical circuit of consciousness itself.

WHEN THE SPIRITUAL BODY IS IMBALANCED

The spiritual layer connects you to higher intelligence — the guiding blueprint that gives life meaning.
When it's blocked or overshadowed by fear, you may feel adrift, cynical, or directionless.
Without that light, the lower bodies lose orientation — like instruments playing without a conductor.

- **Signs:** Lack of purpose, hopelessness, spiritual fatigue, overreliance on external validation.
- **How It Affects the Others:**
  - *Emotional Body:* Emptiness, loss of joy.
  - *Mental Body:* Negativity or disbelief in possibility.
  - *Physical Body:* Low vitality, immune depletion.

When the soul's frequency dims, the whole field forgets its song.

Realignment happens the moment you reconnect — through meditation, prayer, gratitude, nature, or simply stillness.
The light returns, and the lower bodies reorganize around it.

THE DOMINO EFFECT OF DISCONNECTION

Imbalance rarely stays isolated.
A single distorted layer can initiate a chain reaction:

- Emotional stress alters brain chemistry.
- Mental worry disrupts sleep and digestion.
- Physical pain dampens mood and motivation.
- Spiritual disconnection magnifies them all.

Your energy field operates like a living ecosystem — every frequency depends on every other.
This is why one shift in coherence, even a breath, can recalibrate the entire system.
When one instrument begins to play in tune, the others follow.

ENERGETIC INSIGHT

You are the conductor of your four bodies.
Your awareness — not your willpower — is what tunes them.

When imbalance arises, it's not failure; it's *feedback.*
Every misalignment is an invitation to listen, to harmonize, and to restore resonance through awareness.

Heal one layer, and you heal the whole.
Because you were never broken — only out of tune.

"Natural Intelligence is the sacred architecture that AI still seeks to understand."

Exercise: Energy Zone Audit — Identify Your Strongest and Weakest Harmonic

Awareness is the first frequency of transformation. You can't realign what you can't feel.

Purpose

Every person has an **energy signature** — a harmonic blend of emotional, mental, physical, and spiritual frequencies.
When these are balanced, your field vibrates in coherence — your heart, mind, body, and soul sing the same note.
But most people unconsciously "favor" one frequency and underdevelop another.
This exercise helps you discover your natural harmonic pattern: where your energy flows easily, and where it becomes fragmented.

By the end, you'll know your **strongest zone** (your anchor of power) and your **weakest zone** (your area of healing and integration).

Step 1 – Prepare the Field

Find a quiet place.
Sit comfortably with your spine straight, feet grounded, and hands resting on your lap or heart.
Take three slow breaths — in through the nose, out through the mouth.
With each exhale, release the day's static.
With each inhale, invite clarity.

When your mind settles, say inwardly:

"I am ready to listen to my energy with honesty and love."

Step 2 – Tune In to Each Body

You'll scan through all four bodies — emotional, mental, physical, and spiritual — and sense how each feels in this moment.
Use your intuitive channel that's most natural (Visual, Feeler, Knower, or Audio).

1. Emotional Body – The Current of Feeling

Ask: *How freely do my emotions move through me?*

- Do I feel emotions and release them easily, or do I hold them?
- Is my primary vibration lately calm, inspired, anxious, or numb?

Visual: See your emotional energy as color or light.
Feeler: Sense its texture — light, dense, smooth, jagged.
Knower: Simply *know* whether it feels balanced or turbulent.
Audio: Hear it as tone — harmonious or discordant.

Rate it (1–10): how balanced does this layer feel today?

2. Mental Body – The Pattern of Thought

Ask: *What is the rhythm of my mind?*

- Are my thoughts clear and creative or looping and heavy?
- Do my ideas expand possibility or rehearse limitation?

Visual: See your mind as flowing patterns or tangled lines.
Feeler: Notice pressure or ease around the head and neck.
Knower: Sense whether your thoughts feel true or reactive.
Audio: Hear your inner dialogue — encouraging or critical?

Rate this body (1–10).

3. Physical Body – The Ground of Expression

Ask: *How alive does my body feel right now?*

- Is there strength and flow or tension and depletion?
- How is my posture, breath, hydration, or rest?

Visual: Imagine your body's energy as light within each organ or limb.
Feeler: Sense warmth, tingling, or areas of heaviness.
Knower: Trust the quiet knowing of what your body needs most.
Audio: Listen — is your body whispering fatigue or singing vitality?

Rate this body (1–10).

4. Spiritual Body – The Light of Awareness

Ask: *How connected do I feel to my inner guidance or Source today?*

- Do I sense alignment with purpose, or do I feel cut off and uncertain?
- Is my faith in flow or resistance?

Visual: See your spiritual field as radiant light — dim or brilliant.
Feeler: Sense expansion, warmth, or openness in your chest or crown.
Knower: Recognize if truth feels near or distant.
Audio: Listen for inner silence or subtle intuitive whispers.

Rate this body (1–10).

Step 3 – Identify Your Harmonics

Look at your four numbers.

- Your **highest** number is your **strongest harmonic** — the frequency that grounds you.
- Your **lowest** number is your **weakest harmonic** — the area asking for attention.

This doesn't mean something is "wrong."
It means that your system is simply emphasizing one note in the song of your energy — and it's time to bring the rest of the orchestra back in tune.

Step 4 – Interpret the Results

Use this guide for reflection:

Strongest Harmonic	Your Strength	Weakest Harmonic	Your Growth Path
Emotional	Empathy, passion, healing through feeling	Emotional	Practice emotional boundaries and energy release
Mental	Clarity, communication, discernment	Mental	Soften thought control and listen to intuition
Physical	Grounding, embodiment, resilience	Physical	Rest, move, nourish, and strengthen the vessel

Strongest Harmonic	Your Strength	Weakest Harmonic	Your Growth Path
Spiritual	Intuition, higher wisdom, compassion	Spiritual	Anchor purpose into daily physical reality

Step 5 – Harmonize the Field

Close your eyes once more.
Bring awareness to your **weakest harmonic** — the one asking for healing.
Place a hand over the area of your body that feels connected to it (e.g., heart for emotional, head for mental, solar plexus for physical, crown for spiritual).

Now recall the frequency of your **strongest harmonic** — your natural strength.
Let that energy flow through your hand into the weaker area, just as you learned in the *Kinesthetic Touch Method.*
Visualize the strong frequency amplifying the weaker one until they resonate as one sound, one light, one rhythm.

Whisper:

"All my bodies now vibrate as one field of intelligence."

ENERGETIC INSIGHT

This simple audit is your energetic dashboard — a way to read the real-time balance of your inner system.
Over time, you'll notice that your weakest harmonic often reveals your next evolution in consciousness.
As you strengthen it, the others naturally elevate too.

Energy doesn't judge — it calibrates.
Awareness is how you tune your own frequency back to coherence.

"When algorithms learn compassion, we will have achieved true intelligence."

6 | The Zone of Healing Genius Method

You were never meant to chase healing. You were designed to remember it

PHASE 1 – AWARENESS: SEEING THE ENERGY CLEARLY

Everything begins with awareness.
You cannot change what you cannot sense.

Awareness is not mental analysis — it's energetic perception.
It means learning to *see, feel, know, or hear* the subtle information your energy field communicates through emotion, sensation, and synchronicity.

As you develop awareness, you'll begin to notice patterns — the recurring emotional reactions, physical sensations, or thought loops that reveal where energy is stuck.

Ask yourself:

- "What am I feeling in this moment?"
- "Where do I sense it in my body?"
- "What story or memory does this vibration belong to?"

This is the art of energetic observation — witnessing without judgment.

The moment you become aware, you shift from being the pattern to observing it — and that alone begins to reorganize your frequency.

Awareness is light entering the shadow.

PHASE 2 – ACKNOWLEDGMENT: HONORING WHAT ARISES

Once awareness reveals the energy, acknowledgment transforms it. Ignoring, analyzing, or suppressing emotion keeps it looping. Acknowledgment releases it from hiding.

To acknowledge means to **feel without resistance.**
You breathe into the sensation, name the emotion, and accept its message.
You let the energy *exist* without labeling it as good or bad.

This is where many people skip steps — they want to "fix" energy before they've truly felt it.
But healing is not control; it's *communication.*

When you say inwardly,

"Yes, I feel this,"
the emotion softens. The charge begins to dissolve.

Valerie Hunt once said, *"Emotion is the language through which energy reorganizes itself."*
Acknowledgment is how you start that conversation.

PHASE 3 – ACTIVATION: RECONNECTING THE CURRENT

Once the energy is acknowledged, the next step is **activation** — restoring movement where stagnation once lived.

Activation happens through **conscious touch, breath, or visualization.**
You use your body as an instrument to redirect energy — touching one point associated with the emotion (as in your Kinesthetic Touch Method) and another associated with joy, peace, or strength.
Each repetition sends a new message through your nervous system: *"It's safe to feel. It's safe to flow."*

You might notice warmth, tingling, light, or tears — these are signs that energy is being released.

Activation can also occur through sound (chanting, humming, toning), movement (gentle rocking, shaking, stretching), or intention (seeing light move through the body).

Activation is the spark that turns awareness into motion.

It's your "aha" moment not just in mind — but in the body's circuitry.

PHASE 4 – REPATTERNING: REWRITING THE FREQUENCY

Now that the energy is flowing, it's time to **repattern** — to teach your system a new harmonic.

This is where you consciously choose a new emotional frequency to replace the old one.
You can't just "think positive"; you must *embody* a new signal long enough for your brain, heart, and field to memorize it.

Repatterning is done through **repetition of coherent states** — gratitude, compassion, joy, empowerment.
Each time you breathe those emotions into the same place where pain once lived, you overwrite the old energetic software.

Neuroscience calls this *neuroplasticity.*
Energy medicine calls it *vibrational entrainment.*
Spirit calls it *remembering who you are.*

Every breath in coherence reprograms the field of memory.

In this phase, you may find new thoughts emerging — "I am safe now." "I am supported." "I am light."
These are not affirmations; they are *frequencies of truth* resonating through your cells.

PHASE 5 – INTEGRATION: BECOMING THE NEW FREQUENCY

The final phase is **integration** — where healing becomes identity.

You allow the repatterned frequency to stabilize within all four bodies — emotional, mental, physical, and spiritual.
Integration happens through consistent alignment: repeating coherence practices, observing your daily choices, and embodying the new vibration in how you speak, walk, and respond.

It's no longer about managing energy — it's about *living as energy.*

During integration, your outer world begins to mirror the new inner field.
Relationships shift, opportunities appear, synchronicities multiply.
You're no longer seeking healing; you *radiate* it.

Integration is not an ending — it's the embodiment of your genius frequency.

PUTTING IT ALL TOGETHER

Phase	Focus	Practice	Result
1. Awareness	Recognize energy patterns	Observation, journaling, body scanning	Light enters shadow
2. Acknowledgment	Accept what arises	Emotional naming, breath awareness	Release begins
3. Activation	Move the energy	Touch, sound, visualization, breath	Flow returns
4. Repatterning	Teach a new frequency	Coherent emotion, affirmation, rhythm	Memory reprogrammed
5. Integration	Live the new vibration	Daily rituals, coherence practices	Healing becomes creation

"AI may connect systems, but only empathy connects souls."

ENERGETIC INSIGHT

Healing is not an event — it's a frequency evolution.
The *Zone of Healing Genius Method*™ simply provides the structure
that allows that evolution to happen consciously.

As you move through the five phases, you are retraining your entire
field to stay in coherence — to live as the embodiment of genius
itself.

Awareness awakens.
Acknowledgment releases.
Activation restores.
Repatterning rewrites.
Integration radiates.

And this is how you return — not to who you were — but to who
you've always been beneath the noise:
a luminous, intelligent, self-healing being, perfectly attuned to the
rhythm of life.

*"The future healer will not only use data — they will sense
frequency."*

Step-by-Step Kinesthetic Sequence: The Dual-Point Touch

Your body is a living keyboard. Each point you touch is a key that plays the music of your energy.
Touch the pain, touch the peace — then let the song retune itself.

Purpose

The **Dual-Point Touch** bridges the emotional and physical bodies — transforming awareness into movement and coherence.
By touching two points on the body — one that holds tension or emotional charge, and another that represents balance or joy — you **reconnect the circuit** between discord and harmony.
Over time, this reprograms the nervous system to default to coherence instead of chaos.

This is the heart of your *Kinesthetic Repatterning Method* inside *The Zone of Healing Genius™*.

Preparation – Setting the Field

1. **Find a quiet space.**
   Sit or stand comfortably with both feet grounded.
   Let your body feel supported — by the earth, the chair, or your breath.
2. **Center your focus.**
   Place one hand on your heart, the other on your lower abdomen.
   Take three slow, rhythmic breaths (five seconds in, five seconds out).
   As you exhale, imagine releasing static energy.
   As you inhale, imagine breathing in golden light.
3. **State your intention:**

"I am ready to release what no longer serves and reconnect to my natural coherence."

Feel that intention as vibration — not just words.

Step 1 – Identify the Charged Point (Point A)

Scan your body with awareness.
Ask: *Where do I feel discomfort, heaviness, or emotion?*

It may be a physical ache (like the chest, throat, stomach, or back) or an emotional pull (sadness, fear, anger, guilt).
Trust your first instinct — the body never lies.

Gently place one hand over that area.
This is **Point A** — the *frequency of imbalance or stored emotion.*

As you touch it, breathe normally and allow yourself to **feel what's there** without resistance.

Whisper:

"I feel you. I see you. You are safe to exist."

Stay here for 10–20 seconds, simply observing.
You're establishing *awareness and acknowledgment* — Phases 1 and 2 of the Method.

Step 2 – Identify the Harmonizing Point (Point B)

Now, ask: *Where in my body do I feel strong, joyful, or at peace?*
It could be your heart, solar plexus, hands, or even your head.
Wherever the energy feels open, light, or powerful — that's your harmonizing point.

Place your other hand there.
This is **Point B** — the *frequency of coherence.*

You now have one hand on imbalance, one on harmony.
You're physically holding dual aspects of your field — the "problem"
and the "solution" — within your own energy system.

You are the bridge through which energy remembers balance.

Step 3 – Feel the Dual Connection

Close your eyes and breathe deeply, evenly.
Imagine energy flowing between your two hands — from one point
to the other and back again.
Like a current connecting two magnets, you might sense warmth,
tingling, pulsing, or emotional release.

If emotions surface — tears, sighs, laughter — allow them.
Energy is simply moving.
You're completing a circuit that was once disconnected.

Step 4 – Amplify the Coherent Frequency

Now focus on your *harmonizing hand* (Point B).
Recall a powerful emotion of gratitude, love, or joy.
Let that frequency rise in your chest and radiate through that hand.

As you exhale, **send that energy** to the hand resting on Point A —
the one holding the pain.
As you inhale, imagine the harmonized energy being drawn back
through your heart, cleansing the circuit.

Repeat this gentle exchange — exhale peace, inhale restoration —
for about **90 seconds.**

With each cycle, the discord dissolves and the two points begin to feel the same.

You are teaching your nervous system a new emotional truth.

Step 5 – Switch and Integrate

When the energy between the two hands feels balanced — no longer opposing but harmonized — slowly move both hands to your heart.
Breathe deeply three more times.
Imagine the energy field expanding around you — radiant, unified, whole.

Whisper softly:

"The energy has learned a new way to flow.
I am reprogrammed into coherence."

Allow a few seconds of stillness.
Notice what you feel: peace, clarity, warmth, or quiet emptiness.
This is the *Integration Phase* — the new frequency locking into your field.

Optional Expansion: For Advanced Practice

You can use the **Dual-Point Touch** on any level of imbalance — emotional, physical, or spiritual:

- **Emotional:** Touch sadness (heart) and gratitude (solar plexus).
- **Physical:** Touch pain (shoulder) and vitality (abdomen).
- **Spiritual:** Touch confusion (forehead) and faith (crown or heart).

With each session, you strengthen the energy pathways that link pain to peace — teaching your field that coherence is its default setting.

Use this sequence daily for a few minutes or whenever you feel off-balance.
It's a self-healing dialogue between your body and your consciousness.

Scientific & Energetic Context

From a neuroscience perspective, this exercise uses **bilateral stimulation** (similar to EMDR), which helps integrate emotional memory between the brain's hemispheres.
Energetically, it reconnects meridians, balances polarity, and raises the vibrational frequency of the field.
You're literally reprogramming both your biology and your biofield — aligning them in one coherent rhythm.

ENERGETIC INSIGHT

The moment your hands bridge pain and peace, you become the healer — not by force, but by frequency.
Each session refines your field, making coherence easier to access until it becomes your natural state.

Touch is the language of energy.
Awareness is the intelligence that guides it.
You are both.

Reader Reflection: Ask Yourself

Take a moment after completing this practice and ask yourself:

- What sensations or images came forward as I breathed through the shift?
- Where in my body do I feel more open, lighter, or calmer?
- What thought or emotion no longer feels charged?
- What one word describes my new state of coherence right now?

Write your answers in your journal — what you measure, you magnify.

If You're Feeling Overwhelmed...

Transformation can feel like chaos before it becomes creation.
You may notice memories surfacing or emotions intensifying — this is your energy recalibrating.
Don't rush to fix it.
Breathe into your body and remind yourself: *I am safe. I am changing frequencies, not losing control.*
Healing is the art of allowing your light to reorganize itself.

Reader Journal Reflection

Where in my life do I need to reprogram the pattern?

Identify one recurring emotion, reaction, or situation that drains your energy.
What might it look like to respond with coherence instead of conditioning?

"Artificial Intelligence will expand knowledge. Natural Intelligence will expand wisdom."

Case Stories: When the Body "Clicked" Back Into Coherence

There is a moment in every session when the body remembers itself —

a deep breath, a tear, a tremor — and suddenly, coherence returns.

1. THE SHOULDER THAT CARRIED TOO MUCH

Client: *Marina, age 42 — nurse, single mother, constant neck and shoulder pain.*

For months, Marina described her shoulder as "stone." Massage brought no relief.
During her first session, I asked where she felt the weight emotionally.
She touched her shoulder and whispered, "It's where I carry everyone."

We placed one hand there (Point A) and the other on her heart (Point B).
As she breathed, tears began to fall silently. "I never asked for help," she said.
We continued the breath — exhaling love from the heart into the shoulder, inhaling forgiveness back through the chest.

After a few minutes, her shoulder softened under my fingers. She blinked, startled.
"It just *clicked*," she said. "It doesn't hurt."
What had shifted wasn't muscle — it was memory. The body had stopped holding the story of burden.

When she allowed herself to feel supported, her body released the need to hold.

2. THE GRIEF BENEATH THE STOMACH ACHE

Client: *Evan, 36 — entrepreneur, stomach pain, sleeplessness, and anxiety.*

He insisted it was "just stress," but his abdomen pulsed with trapped emotion.
We began with awareness — one hand over the gut, the other over the solar plexus.
When asked what emotion lived there, he paused. "Loss," he said softly. His father had died three years earlier, and he had never cried.

We activated the Dual-Point Touch.
On the exhale, he sent compassion from his solar plexus to his stomach; on the inhale, he drew peace back in.
After two minutes, his breath deepened, and his face relaxed.
"I can finally feel him," he said — not as pain, but as warmth.

Grief had not left; it had transformed into love. That is coherence.

3. THE VOICE THAT COULDN'T SPEAK

Client: *Tessa, 29 — singer who had lost her voice after an emotional breakup.*

The doctors found no physical damage. "It's psychological," they said.
We began at the throat (Point A) and heart (Point B).
When she touched her throat, she whispered, "I never said goodbye."

As she breathed through both points, I guided her to hum softly on the exhale.
At first, it was barely audible — then, suddenly, her voice cracked

open, full of vibration.
Her eyes widened. "I can feel it — the sound came from my heart!"

Her voice returned not through effort, but through reconnection.

The moment she let love speak through her, her body remembered how to sing.

4. THE MIND THAT WOULDN'T STOP

Client: *Sanjay, 50 — engineer, insomniac, constant mental chatter.*

When asked what he felt in his body, he said, "Nothing — just thoughts."
We began with his forehead (Point A) and his chest (Point B).
I asked him to imagine his thoughts as clouds and his heart as the sky beneath them.

As he touched both points and breathed, something subtle changed.
His jaw softened, his eyes moistened. "I feel a pulse in my chest," he said, astonished.
After several rounds, he whispered, "The thoughts are still there, but they don't *matter.*"

When the brain entrains to the rhythm of the heart, noise becomes silence.

He slept deeply that night — for the first time in months.

5. THE WOMAN WHO REMEMBERED LIGHT

Client: *Adriana, 67 — long-term depression after losing her spouse.*

She arrived hollow, her energy dim. We started gently: one hand on her heart, one on her crown.

I guided her to recall a moment of pure joy — she remembered dancing barefoot in her garden years ago.

With each breath, we amplified that memory, letting it pour through her hands.
Her body began to sway slightly. "I see gold light," she whispered. "It's moving."
After the session, her face glowed — the dullness replaced by presence.

Her vibration had returned. The light she thought she lost was simply waiting for recognition.

A week later, she wrote:

"I don't know if I'm healed, but I'm *alive.* I can feel again."

ENERGETIC REFLECTION

Every story ends differently — one with a sigh, another with a smile —

but the turning point is always the same: the **click of coherence.**
It's that instant when energy reorganizes, the nervous system stops bracing, and the heart and brain pulse as one.

This is not magic — it's remembrance.
The body isn't being *fixed*; it's being *reminded.*

Healing doesn't happen when you force the body to change.
It happens when you let it remember the truth of its rhythm.

Practice: The Five-Minute Daily Repattern

Coherence isn't a moment — it's a muscle.
Train it daily, and your energy will remember how to stay in harmony.

Purpose

This five-minute ritual reprograms your nervous system and energy field for coherence every day.
Think of it as your "frequency hygiene" — like brushing your energy body clean each morning or evening.
It teaches your mind, heart, and body to stay synchronized, even amid stress, uncertainty, or change.

You can do it sitting, standing, or lying down — anywhere you can place both hands on your body.

THE SEQUENCE (FIVE MINUTES TOTAL)
1. Minute One – Awareness (Breathe + Scan)

Objective: Identify your current state.

- Close your eyes and breathe slowly, evenly, for a count of **five in, five out.**
- Ask yourself:

  "What am I feeling right now?"
  "Where do I feel it in my body?"

- Let the first response come — don't overthink.

Visual learners: Imagine your energy body as colored light — where is it dim or dense?
Feelers: Notice temperature, tension, or flow.
Knowers: Sense instantly what's off.
Audios: Listen inwardly for tone — is it smooth or chaotic?

This is your **Point A** — the location of the old pattern.

2. Minute Two – Acknowledgment (Touch + Name)

Objective: Honor the emotion or energy present.

Place one hand gently on that area.
Whisper inwardly:

"I see you. I feel you. You are safe to exist."

Allow the emotion to be fully *felt* — whether sadness, irritation, fear, or numbness.
Feeling *is* the beginning of release.

Tip: The body heals fastest when it's heard.

3. Minute Three – Activation (Dual-Point Touch)

Objective: Connect the circuit between imbalance and harmony.

Find your **Point B** — a spot in your body that feels peaceful, strong, or joyful.
Place your other hand there.

Now breathe in through your nose, exhale through your mouth.
Visualize light traveling between both hands — a current of energy connecting the two points.

Each exhale sends calm, love, or strength from the harmonious point into the tense one.
Each inhale draws peace back through your heart.

Stay with this gentle rhythm for about one minute, allowing energy to equalize.

This is your personal energy reset — one breath, one bridge, one frequency.

4. Minute Four – Repatterning (Choose + Anchor)

Objective: Install the new coherent frequency.

Move both hands to your heart.
Recall a memory that fills you with gratitude, joy, or love — a moment that makes your entire body smile.
Feel that emotion until it expands beyond your chest, radiating through your entire field.

Now speak your chosen frequency aloud or silently:

"I choose peace."
"I choose trust."
"I choose vitality."

Whatever truth feels right — let it become your **new energetic imprint.**

5. Minute Five – Integration (Breathe + Radiate)

Objective: Lock the new pattern into your system.

Stay still for the final minute.
Imagine your body surrounded by a soft golden or white light —

coherent, calm, intelligent.
See that light expanding six feet in all directions, filling your aura.

Say softly:

"This is my frequency.
My heart and mind are one rhythm.
My body is light in motion."

Take one final deep breath.
Open your eyes and notice:

- Is your breath slower?
- Is your body lighter?
- Has your perception shifted?

Even subtle changes mean your energy has "clicked" back into coherence.

Make It a Habit

For best results:

- **Morning:** Do it before checking your phone or starting work — it sets your vibration for the day.
- **Evening:** Repeat before bed — it clears the field for deep rest and overnight healing.
- **Anytime stress hits:** Take 90 seconds to reconnect; coherence happens faster with practice.

This is how you reprogram your baseline frequency from reactive to radiant.

Five minutes a day changes your vibration — and your vibration changes everything.

ENERGETIC INSIGHT

Every repetition of this ritual strengthens your heart–brain rhythm, balances your electromagnetic field, and deepens your trust in inner intelligence.
After a few weeks, your body will start doing it automatically — pausing, breathing, recalibrating — without you needing to think about it.

That is true reprogramming.
That is **living in your Zone of Healing Genius.**

"Artificial Intelligence can process data. Natural Intelligence can perceive meaning. The future of healing depends on both."

7 | Breaking the Energy Thieves

Your energy is sacred currency.
Every thought, every emotion, every choice either invests it or leaks it.

The Four Primary Drains

No matter how skilled you become at coherence, if your field leaks energy, you'll keep falling out of alignment.
The greatest leaks aren't physical — they're emotional.
They come disguised as moral virtues, hidden patterns of self-sabotage that keep your vibration just below your true potential.

I call them **the Energy Thieves**:

1. **Guilt** – the thief of worthiness.
2. **Resentment** – the thief of peace.
3. **Perfectionism** – the thief of flow.
4. **Fear** – the thief of freedom.

Each of these emotions creates energetic "drag" in your field — lowering frequency, weakening your coherence, and distorting your electromagnetic rhythm.
The more often you engage with them, the more they program your nervous system for depletion instead of creation.

The good news?
Once you *see* them, you can reclaim the energy they've been stealing — and redirect it toward your genius.

1. GUILT — THE THIEF OF WORTHINESS

Frequency signature: heavy, downward-pulling, self-punishing.
Energy pattern: "I did something wrong."

Guilt convinces you that suffering is payment for being human.
It makes you shrink your light because you believe you don't deserve to shine.
Energetically, guilt creates a low-frequency loop between the solar plexus and the heart — your personal power and self-love centers.

When guilt runs the show, your field closes; coherence collapses.
The body often feels pressure in the chest, nausea, or fatigue in the gut.

The Repattern:
Touch your solar plexus (Point A) and your heart (Point B).
Breathe and repeat:

"I am forgiven. I am free. I am worthy of my light."

Each repetition restores your power to innocence — not because you've earned it, but because worthiness was never lost.

Forgiveness is the highest frequency antidote to guilt.

2. RESENTMENT — THE THIEF OF PEACE

Frequency signature: sharp, fiery, contracted.
Energy pattern: "They hurt me, and I can't let it go."

Resentment keeps you tied to the very energy you want to escape.
It locks your frequency in the past, replaying scenes of injustice and
betrayal like an energetic echo.
In the body, resentment often shows up as tension in the liver,
shoulders, and jaw — the body literally "grinding" on unexpressed
anger.

Energetically, it sends out incoherent waves that destabilize your
field.
Even if your heart wants to heal, resentment keeps the circuit open
to pain.

The Repattern:
Touch your jaw or liver area (Point A) and your heart (Point B).
As you breathe, whisper:

"I release the past. I choose peace. I reclaim my energy."

Visualize the person or memory dissolving into light — not to
condone what happened, but to *set your field free.*

*Forgiveness doesn't excuse the behavior — it ends your energetic
contract with it.*

3. PERFECTIONISM — THE THIEF OF FLOW

Frequency signature: tight, anxious, brittle.
Energy pattern: "It's never enough — I'm never enough."

Perfectionism masquerades as excellence, but it's really fear in disguise.
It drains life-force by keeping your energy stuck in the mental body, looping between judgment and control.
The more you strive, the more your nervous system stays in survival mode — producing cortisol instead of creativity.

Physically, you may feel constriction in the throat, shallow breathing, or tension in the back of the neck.
Energetically, your flow becomes rigid; intuition can't enter a system that refuses imperfection.

The Repattern:
Touch your forehead (Point A) and your heart (Point B).
Breathe deeply and say:

"I am enough as I am.
I create from joy, not from fear."

With each breath, imagine the perfectionist voice dissolving into laughter — the universal sound of freedom.

Flow requires permission to be human.

4. FEAR — THE THIEF OF FREEDOM

Frequency signature: cold, contracting, paralyzing.
Energy pattern: "Something bad is coming."

Fear is the oldest survival program. It shuts down the creative centers of the brain, floods the body with adrenaline, and collapses the heart field.
But fear itself isn't the enemy — it's information.
When acknowledged, it becomes fuel for awareness.
When denied, it becomes a cage.

The vibration of fear pulls the energy field inward — shrinking your aura, limiting intuition, and freezing possibility.

The Repattern:
Touch your root (lower abdomen or hips) (Point A) and your heart (Point B).
Breathe slowly, lengthening the exhale.
Say:

"I am safe in this moment.
I trust the intelligence of life."

With every exhale, see your field expanding — red at the root, green at the heart — merging into gold light.
That gold is courage: fear transformed through love.

Courage isn't the absence of fear; it's the frequency that moves through it.

THE ENERGETIC MATHEMATICS OF DRAINING AND RECLAIMING

Each of these thieves drains energy because it pulls your vibration away from coherence — fragmenting the four bodies of intelligence.

Energy Thief	Affected Bodies	Repatterned Frequency	Restored Field
Guilt	Emotional + Solar Plexus	Forgiveness	Worthiness
Resentment	Emotional + Liver/Throat	Compassion	Peace
Perfectionism	Mental + Throat	Acceptance	Flow
Fear	Physical + Root	Trust	Freedom

Every time you shift one of these frequencies, you reclaim measurable vitality in your field.

Dr. Valerie Hunt's biofield research showed that forgiveness, acceptance, and trust generate higher electromagnetic amplitudes — literally *stronger light*.

MINI PRACTICE – THE FOUR-POINT RELEASE

1. Place a hand over your **heart.**
2. Recall which thief has been draining you most today.
3. Touch the corresponding body area (gut for guilt, liver for resentment, throat for perfectionism, root for fear).
4. Take three slow breaths and say:

   "I reclaim my energy from this pattern.
   My field is whole. My light is restored."

Feel the shift — the warmth, calm, or expansion that signals your energy has come home.

ENERGETIC INSIGHT

You cannot stay in your **Zone of Healing Genius** while leaking energy into guilt, resentment, perfectionism, or fear.
But once you reclaim those fragments, your field stabilizes in coherence.
The heart leads. The mind follows. The body relaxes. The soul expands.

Every leak you seal becomes power you can use to create.
Every pattern you release becomes light you can radiate.

And that — right there — is the true meaning of healing genius

"When energy and information merge through consciousness,
healing becomes creation."

How to Transmute Emotional Density into Vitality

Emotions don't disappear when ignored — they change form.
When transformed consciously, density becomes power.

THE ALCHEMY OF ENERGY

Every emotion carries a vibration.
Low-frequency emotions — grief, anger, guilt, fear — are simply **slower-moving energy waves** that condense in the body as tension, fatigue, or pain.
High-frequency emotions — gratitude, joy, love, peace — are **faster-moving waves** that create expansion, radiance, and vitality.

Neither is "good" or "bad."
They are *different states of the same energy*.

When you feel a heavy emotion and meet it with resistance, you trap the energy in your tissues — it becomes *density*.
When you feel it with presence, breath, and awareness, the vibration begins to move again — it becomes *vitality*.

Density is frozen light. Presence is the heat that melts it.

This is emotional alchemy — not rejecting emotion, but transforming it into life-force.

WHY THE BODY STORES EMOTIONAL DENSITY

The nervous system's primary job is safety.
When a situation overwhelms your ability to process emotion in the moment, the body "quarantines" that energy — holding it in

muscles, fascia, or organs until you're ready to face it.
This is a survival mechanism, not failure.

But stored emotion consumes enormous energy.
It demands constant vigilance — subconscious muscular tension, hormonal vigilance, and mental loops to keep the "storage tank" sealed.
That's why unresolved emotion leads to fatigue, pain, and disconnection.

The moment you bring awareness and breath to that storage, the nervous system recognizes safety — and releases the energy back into circulation as vitality.

The emotion you're most afraid to feel contains the most energy waiting to be freed.

STEP-BY-STEP TRANSMUTATION PRACTICE

(Integrate this with your daily coherence or Dual-Point Touch practice.)

Step 1 – Locate the Density

Close your eyes and scan your body.
Where do you feel tightness, heaviness, or pressure?
That's the doorway.
Don't analyze it — simply acknowledge: *"There is energy here."*

This is the **first law of transmutation** — *what you resist, persists; what you face, dissolves.*

Step 2 – Name the Frequency

Ask yourself:

"If this sensation had an emotion, what would it be?"

Is it fear? Grief? Shame? Anger? Sadness?
Naming the emotion begins to loosen its charge because the conscious mind is now in relationship with it.

If you can't name it, that's okay — simply describe it through sensation: *heavy, cold, buzzing, dull, tight.*
The key is observation without judgment.

Step 3 – Add Breath and Compassion

Breathe into that space as though your breath were light entering a cave.
On each inhale, imagine warmth filling the area.
On each exhale, imagine the heaviness softening, loosening, dissolving.

Place your hand over that point if it helps (Point A).
Then place your other hand on your heart (Point B).

Now you're linking the **site of density** to the **frequency of compassion** — the same current that powers coherence.

Stay with it for 90 seconds.
Notice when the emotion shifts — from tightness to tingling, from tears to calm.
That shift *is* the transmutation.

Step 4 – Raise the Frequency

Once the emotion starts to move, consciously invite in a higher vibration:
Gratitude, love, joy, forgiveness — whatever feels authentic.

Say aloud or inwardly:

"I choose to raise this energy to its highest form."

Visualize the once-heavy emotion rising through your heart and out through your crown as golden or white light.
You may even feel a surge of warmth or electricity — that's vitality returning to the system.

You haven't "lost" energy — you've upgraded it.

Step 5 – Anchor the Vitality

Finally, imagine that golden energy flowing through your bloodstream, nourishing every cell.
Feel it radiate from your skin.
Smile softly — the body knows this frequency as home.

Whisper:

"This emotion has become light.
I am charged, coherent, and alive."

Take a moment of silence to savor the peace — the calm that follows the storm of release.

THE SCIENCE OF TRANSMUTATION

Neuroscientifically, this process shifts the body from sympathetic (fight-flight) dominance to parasympathetic (rest-heal) coherence. Heart rate variability (HRV) increases, cortisol drops, and oxytocin rises — signaling the body that it's safe to restore and repair.

Energetically, the electromagnetic field around the heart expands, measurable by devices like HeartMath's sensors.
Dr. Valerie Hunt observed this as a visible increase in light amplitude in the biofield during emotional release.
It's not metaphor — **it's measurable.**

"The New Paradigm of Healing is not about replacing humanity with technology, but harmonizing the two into one intelligent field."

EMOTIONAL ALCHEMY MAP

Emotion (Density)	Frequency in Hz (Approximate)	Transmuted Vitality	New State of Being
Guilt / Shame	20–50 Hz	Forgiveness	Worthiness
Anger / Resentment	150–200 Hz	Compassion	Peace
Fear / Anxiety	100–150 Hz	Trust	Freedom
Grief / Sadness	75–100 Hz	Love	Connection
Apathy / Numbness	<20 Hz	Gratitude	Aliveness

(Note: Frequencies derived from general vibrational models used in bioenergetics and emotional resonance research.)

ENERGETIC INSIGHT

Emotional density isn't your enemy — it's compressed potential. Every time you feel and transform it, your frequency rises, your vitality expands, and your Genius Field strengthens.

Feeling is transmutation.
Breath is the fire.
Awareness is the alchemist.

This is not bypassing emotion; it's metabolizing it into life-force. The energy you reclaim from density is the same energy you'll use to heal, create, love, and serve.

The deeper you're willing to feel, the higher you're able to rise.

Practice: Energy Detox — Release, Refill, Radiate

You cleanse your body with water — now cleanse your energy with light.

Purpose

This 7–10 minute ritual resets your entire biofield, helping you release emotional residue, refill with coherent energy, and radiate your highest frequency into your environment.
It can be done in the morning (to start clear and grounded) or evening (to clear accumulated emotional density).

Each step aligns with the **3 phases of energetic purification**:

1. **Release** – Let go of what no longer serves your field.
2. **Refill** – Recharge with coherent, high-frequency energy.
3. **Radiate** – Expand that energy outward into your life.

This practice combines **breath, visualization, touch, and frequency** to create a deep detox — emotionally, mentally, physically, and spiritually.

Step 1: RELEASE — Clear the Static

Before you can rise in frequency, you must empty what's full of noise.

1. **Ground the Body.**
   Stand or sit tall, feet flat, spine straight.
   Imagine roots extending from your feet deep into the earth.
   Feel gravity pulling away everything heavy — worry, fatigue, anger, guilt.
2. **Scan the Field.**
   Bring awareness from head to toe.

Sense any tension, emotion, or thought that feels heavy or stuck.
Visualize these areas as gray or dark static in your aura.

3. **Exhale to Purge.**
Inhale slowly through your nose.
On each exhale, blow out the static through your mouth — releasing energy from the chest, shoulders, and belly.
Imagine the gray mist leaving your field and dissolving into the earth to be neutralized.

4. **Optional Kinesthetic Add-On:**
   - Use both hands to "sweep" around your body, brushing off the energy field from head to knees.
   - Shake out your hands or arms to discharge excess energy.

Whisper:

"I release all frequencies that are not mine.
My energy is clear, calm, and light."

Stay here until you feel space opening — a lightness in the body, a softening in the breath, or an inner quiet.

Step 2: REFILL — Recharge with Coherence

You don't fight darkness — you turn on the light.

1. **Connect to the Heart.**
Place both hands over your chest.
Breathe into your heart center for a count of 5 in, 5 out.
Feel warmth building beneath your palms — this is your coherent core activating.

2. **Draw in Light.**
On each inhale, imagine drawing pure golden-white energy down from above your head.

See it entering through your crown, filling your spine, and flowing into every organ and cell.

3. **Amplify the Emotion.**

Recall a memory of gratitude, love, or joy.

Feel that emotion expanding through your heart until your entire body glows with it.

4. **Dual-Point Refill (Optional).**

Place one hand on your heart (Point A) and one on your lower abdomen (Point B).

Breathe light between the two — harmonizing your upper and lower energy centers.

Whisper:

"My heart refills me with coherent light.
My body is nourished with love and peace."

Stay in this feeling for 2–3 minutes.
Notice the shift — from hollow to full, from tired to radiant.

Step 3: RADIATE — Expand the Field

Energy not shared becomes stagnant. Radiance completes the circuit.

1. **Expand the Light.**

Imagine your heart as a radiant sun.

With every breath, see its light expanding beyond your chest — through your aura, into the room, the sky, the earth.

Feel the glow around you pulsing with calm power.

2. **Send Coherence Outward.**

Picture this light touching everyone you love, then the people you struggle with, then the entire planet.

You're not giving energy away — you're amplifying coherence through resonance.

3. **Set the Intention.**
   Whisper or say aloud:

   "May my energy uplift all who feel it.
   May my light harmonize the spaces I enter.
   May coherence ripple through me and beyond me."

4. **Seal the Field.**
   Visualize your aura now as a golden sphere — strong, clear, and luminous.
   It allows love to flow in and out, but blocks chaos and distortion.

Stay in silence for a few breaths, basking in the peace you've created.

The Physiology Behind the Detox

- **Release:** Activates parasympathetic response; cortisol drops, muscle tension decreases.
- **Refill:** Raises oxytocin and serotonin; expands the heart's electromagnetic amplitude.
- **Radiate:** Entrains surrounding fields into coherence — measurable through HeartMath studies of energetic synchronization.

Energetically, you are flushing out low-frequency charge, restoring pranic flow, and expanding the Genius Field around you.
You are becoming a transmitter of coherence.

ENERGETIC INSIGHT

Every emotion you release becomes pure life-force when met with love.
Every breath you take with intention adds wattage to your light.
Every time you radiate peace, you rewrite the frequency of the collective field.

Energy detox isn't escape — it's remembrance.
You were never meant to hold pain — only to transform it into light.

Do this practice daily or anytime your energy feels dense, cloudy, or overstimulated.
You'll notice a pattern: the more you release, the faster you refill, and the farther you radiate.

That is coherence in motion.
That is the rhythm of your **Zone of Healing Genius.**

"AI will decode emotion through patterns.
The heart decodes it through presence."

8 | Installing Your New Frequency

Healing isn't complete when you feel better — it's complete when your energy knows the way back on its own.

WHY INSTALLATION MATTERS

You've released, repatterned, and recalibrated your energy.
Now, it's time to **stabilize** your new vibration so it becomes your natural default — not a temporary state you "visit."

Most people experience moments of coherence and insight, but they slip back into old patterns because their **neural and energetic circuits** haven't yet learned to *sustain* the new frequency.

Installation is about *teaching your field consistency.*
Just like a new song must be played over and over before it becomes muscle memory, a new vibration must be practiced until the body and mind recognize it as home.

You're not trying to change who you are — you're training your biology to match who you've become.

The Science of Neural Anchoring

The brain is a pattern-recognition organ.
Every time you repeat a thought, emotion, or behavior, neurons wire together to form a **pathway** — a shortcut that makes future repetition easier.
This is called **Hebbian learning:** "Neurons that fire together, wire together."

When you practice coherence daily — through touch, breath, or emotion — you're reassigning those neural pathways from stress to serenity.
Each time your heart and brain synchronize, the vagus nerve signals safety, the amygdala quiets, and your prefrontal cortex (the seat of higher insight) activates.

Over time, this rewiring changes your **baseline vibration.**
Instead of reacting to stress, your system begins to regulate from within.

Repetition builds reality.
Every coherent moment is a rep in your energetic gym.

THE PHYSICS OF ENERGETIC ANCHORING

On an energetic level, repetition creates **resonance** — the process by which a frequency strengthens itself through consistent vibration.
When you hold a coherent emotion like gratitude or love for even two minutes, the electromagnetic field around your heart expands exponentially — up to three feet wider than in a neutral state.

Dr. Valerie Hunt's research demonstrated that when coherent emotions were practiced repeatedly, the body's biofield maintained elevated light amplitude for hours afterward — even without

conscious effort.
This means your **energy learns**.

Just as sound waves stabilize a tone in a tuning fork, emotional and energetic repetition stabilizes your personal frequency.
You're literally entraining your field into coherence.

The more often you visit coherence, the easier it finds you.

HOW THE TWO SYSTEMS SYNC

Level	Mechanism	What Happens	Result
Neural	Repetition of coherent states rewires brain pathways	Stress patterns weaken; safety patterns strengthen	Calm focus and creativity
Energetic	Resonance builds through consistent emotional frequency	Field amplitude increases; coherence stabilizes	Stronger intuition and vitality
Spiritual	Conscious intention anchors purpose	Light body harmonizes with higher intelligence	Embodied awareness and faith

The key is *repetition with emotion*.
Emotion charges thought with energy — the fuel that imprints both neurons and the field.
This is why empty affirmations don't work — but gratitude, awe, and love change everything.

When the mind thinks, and the heart feels the same thought, the universe listens.

PRACTICE: THE FREQUENCY ANCHOR RITUAL

Each repetition is a declaration: "This is who I am now."

1. **Choose Your Frequency Word.**
    Pick one word that represents the vibration you're ready to live from — *Peace, Trust, Radiance, Joy, Freedom, Flow, Love.*

2. **Set a Touchpoint.**
    Choose a simple physical gesture (hand on heart, fingers touching thumb, or palm over solar plexus).
    This gesture becomes your **neural anchor** — linking body and frequency.

3. **Breathe It In.**
    Close your eyes, place your hand on the anchor point, and breathe slowly.
    On each inhale, imagine drawing your chosen frequency into every cell.
    On each exhale, imagine releasing everything that doesn't match it.

4. **Add Emotion.**
    Feel the frequency — not as a concept, but as a sensation.
    If your word is *Peace*, feel the softness of calm water.
    If it's *Joy*, feel the warmth of sunlight in your chest.
    If it's *Freedom*, feel your energy expanding outward.

5. **Repeat for 2–3 Minutes.**
    Whisper your word with each breath:

    "Peace in... Peace out."
    "Love in... Love out."

6. **Anchor the Memory.**
    When you open your eyes, do your physical gesture again and say:

"This is my frequency now."

Each time you repeat this ritual — in the car, before sleep, before a meeting — your system strengthens the neural and energetic connection.

After about **21 days**, your body begins to default to this vibration automatically.

ENERGETIC INSIGHT

Installation is not about control; it's about *consistency.*
You are no longer chasing states — you are cultivating stability.

When you reach this level, life's challenges no longer "knock you off balance."
They simply become opportunities to reaffirm coherence.

Healing becomes identity.
Frequency becomes foundation.

You are now living *inside* the Zone of Healing Genius — not visiting it.
Your thoughts, emotions, and field are tuned to the same rhythm: one of peace, creation, and power.

This is how genius is installed — not by thinking differently, but by vibrating differently long enough for the world to reflect it back.

"In the medicine of the future, coherence will be the new vital sign."

Creating Physical, Emotional, and Environmental Anchors

Your energy becomes stable when your world reflects it back to you.

WHY ANCHORS MATTER

You've learned how to raise your frequency — now it's time to make it *stay.*

Anchors are physical, emotional, and environmental cues that remind your nervous system and energy field:

"This is who I am now."

They turn invisible vibration into visible structure.
Anchors help the body *remember* coherence even when the mind forgets.
Over time, these subtle signals become automatic — your world itself becomes your healing environment.

An anchor is anything that holds your frequency steady during life's waves.

1. Physical Anchors — Teaching the Body the Language of Light

The body learns through movement, touch, and repetition.
When you create physical rituals linked to your new vibration, you train your cells to associate coherence with tangible sensation.

Ideas for Physical Anchors:

- **Touch Gesture:**
  Your hand-to-heart gesture (used in the Frequency Anchor Ritual) becomes your instant reset.

Every time you touch that point, your nervous system recalls calm and coherence.

- **Object of Resonance:**
Carry or wear something infused with intention — a crystal, pendant, essential oil, or ring you touch when reconnecting to your frequency.
These are not "lucky charms" — they are symbolic switches, storing emotional charge through repetition.

- **Body Movement:**
Pair your frequency with a motion:
    - A deep breath with arms opening wide (Freedom).
    - A bow of gratitude with hands to heart (Peace).
    - A slow stretch with a smile (Joy).
    Movement imprints energy in muscle memory.

- **Breath Pattern:**
Use one breath rhythm as your signature frequency anchor — for instance, *inhale 5, exhale 5.*
The brain associates that rhythm with safety and coherence.

When your body moves in the rhythm of coherence, your field follows.

2. Emotional Anchors — Teaching the Heart Its Signature Frequency

Emotions are magnetic — they attract experiences that match their vibration.
To maintain coherence, you must cultivate **emotional familiarity** with your chosen frequency.

Ideas for Emotional Anchors:

- **Gratitude Practice:**
Each morning, recall *one specific* thing that fills you with genuine gratitude — not general thankfulness, but a

memory that makes your chest warm.
This builds emotional muscle for coherence.

- **Music as Emotion:**
Choose one or two songs that instantly raise your vibration.
Play them when you feel low; let your heart entrain to the rhythm of the sound.
Music is frequency medicine — it organizes your biofield through harmony.

- **Scent and Emotion:**
Use aromatherapy as a fast emotional anchor.
Each essential oil has a vibrational signature:
  - Lavender for peace
  - Citrus for joy
  - Frankincense for spiritual connection
  - Rose for love
    Inhale your chosen scent as you focus on your frequency word.

- **Emotional Tagging:**
When something beautiful happens, pause and *name the feeling out loud*:
"This is what freedom feels like."
"This is what peace feels like."
By naming it, you tell your brain: *remember this pattern.*

Your emotional field is your compass — train it to point toward joy.

3. Environmental Anchors — Teaching Your World to Mirror Your Energy

The space you live and work in constantly feeds information to your energy field.
Clutter, harsh lighting, and chaotic sound scatter your frequency.
Intention, beauty, and nature stabilize it.

Ideas for Environmental Anchors:

- **Sacred Space:**
  Designate a small area in your home — even a corner of a table — as your *frequency altar.*
  Include items that represent coherence: a candle, a crystal, a symbol of light, or a written affirmation of your chosen frequency word.
  Visit it daily for a few breaths.
- **Color and Light:**
  Surround yourself with colors that match your desired vibration:
  - Soft greens and pinks for love.
  - Blues for clarity and peace.
  - Golds and whites for illumination.
  - Earth tones for grounding.
    Light candles or use gentle, warm lighting at night to signal safety to the body.
- **Soundscape:**
  Play soft instrumental or ambient music that resonates with your energy.
  Avoid prolonged silence if it amplifies mental noise; instead, fill your space with frequencies that soothe.
- **Decluttering as Detox:**
  Each object holds energetic residue.
  Periodically clear your space — not just for tidiness, but to keep the field clear.
  When you remove what's stagnant, you make room for flow.
- **Nature as Calibration:**
  Spend time outside daily.
  Nature's resonance — Schumann frequency of ~7.83 Hz — is the Earth's coherence signal.
  Walking barefoot on grass or breathing ocean air instantly resets your electromagnetic rhythm.

Your environment is not neutral — it's either draining you or training you.

Putting It All Together

Anchor Type	Example	Frequency Benefit
Physical	Touch to heart, breath pattern, jewelry	Trains body memory for coherence
Emotional	Gratitude, scent, music	Strengthens heart–brain rhythm
Environmental	Sacred space, color, sound, declutter	Keeps outer world aligned with inner frequency

Each anchor reinforces the others.
Your body remembers through sensation.
Your heart remembers through emotion.
Your environment remembers through reflection.

When all three align, you live in a *feedback loop of coherence.*

You are no longer trying to "stay high-vibe."
You are surrounded by reminders that you already are.

ENERGETIC INSIGHT

Anchors aren't props — they are extensions of your consciousness.
When you assign meaning to something, you give it magnetic charge.
Every time you engage with it, that charge amplifies.

A ring becomes protection when blessed with intention.
A candle becomes prayer when lit with awareness.
A breath becomes medicine when taken with love.

As your physical, emotional, and environmental worlds synchronize, your field becomes stable, radiant, and self-sustaining.
You no longer rely on fleeting motivation — you live inside an ecosystem of coherence.

That is mastery.
That is **installation complete.**

"We are not learning to become machines;
we are remembering that we are light."

Morning & Evening Frequency Reset Rituals

How you begin and end each day determines the vibration you live in between.

Purpose

Every night, your consciousness resets.
Every morning, you awaken with a choice:

"Which frequency will I live from today?"

And every evening, you have another choice:

"Which frequency will I carry into my dreams?"

These two small rituals — one at sunrise, one before rest — are your daily tuning forks.
They keep your vibration clear, your nervous system coherent, and your Genius Field active 24 hours a day.

Five minutes morning + five minutes night = a lifetime of coherence.

MORNING FREQUENCY RESET — "TUNE THE FIELD"

Begin your day in coherence, and the universe will match your rhythm.

1. Wake in Stillness (Awareness Phase)

Before checking your phone or moving too quickly, keep your eyes closed.
Place your hand over your heart.

Take **three slow breaths** — in through your nose, out through your mouth.

Ask softly:

"What energy am I waking up with today?"

Notice the tone of your field — calm, heavy, excited, anxious — without judgment.
Awareness alone begins to organize the energy.

2. Anchor Intention (Acknowledgment Phase)

Whisper or write:

"Today I choose to live as [your frequency word]."
(e.g., Peace, Freedom, Love, Flow, Radiance, Joy)

Say it until it *feels true* in your chest.
You are acknowledging your power to create coherence before the day begins.

3. Activate the Body (Activation Phase)

Sit up and place one hand on your **heart** and one on your **navel** (the core power center).
Inhale through your heart, exhale through your abdomen.
Repeat for about a minute, imagining energy flowing up and down — connecting heart and body, thought and action.

Visualize your body lighting up like a sunrise.
This breath sets your electromagnetic field into coherent rhythm.

4. Speak the New Frequency (Repatterning Phase)

Say aloud:

"I radiate [frequency word].
Every thought, word, and choice aligns with this energy today."

Smile gently as you speak — smiling tells the brain, *It's safe to believe this.*

If you prefer sound, hum or chant softly for 20–30 seconds — the vibration through the chest stabilizes your heart rhythm.

5. Seal the Field (Integration Phase)

Stand and stretch.
Visualize a sphere of golden light expanding around you — about six feet in every direction.
Say:

"My field is clear, strong, and radiant.
Only energy that matches my frequency may enter."

Take one final deep breath.
When you open your eyes, move slowly into your day as if your aura were still glowing.

This is your vibrational armor — built not from defense, but from coherence.

"When consciousness becomes coherent, creation responds instantly."

EVENING FREQUENCY RESET — "RETURN TO LIGHT"

The energy you take into sleep becomes tomorrow's starting frequency.

1. Unplug from the Noise (Awareness Phase)

Before bed, dim the lights.
Put away electronics.
Take a slow walk around your space — noticing what energy the day left behind.

Ask yourself:

"What am I still carrying that isn't mine?"

Awareness clears the clutter.

2. Release the Day (Acknowledgment + Activation Phase)

Sit or lie down.
Place one hand over your heart, one over your lower abdomen.
Inhale through the nose, exhale through the mouth.
As you exhale, imagine releasing every emotion, conversation, or thought that doesn't serve your peace.

You may visualize gray mist leaving your body or imagine the earth gently absorbing the day's static.

Whisper:

"I release the day. I am safe to rest."

If tension remains, lightly sweep your hands over your aura from head to feet — clearing the field.

3. Refill with Light (Repatterning Phase)

Now, imagine breathing in soft golden light through your crown.
See it filling your body from head to toe, soothing every cell.
Let gratitude rise — recall one moment from today that felt aligned, kind, or meaningful.

Breathe that gratitude into your heart for 30–60 seconds.
This emotion reprograms your nervous system overnight.

Gratitude while falling asleep is the most healing frequency the body can know.

4. Radiate to Rest (Integration Phase)

Visualize your heart glowing brighter with each breath until it radiates beyond your skin.
Say:

"I rest in coherence.
I sleep in light.
I awaken renewed."

Imagine yourself floating in a field of soft light — safe, supported, infinite.
As you drift into sleep, feel your breath and heartbeat syncing into one rhythm — the rhythm of creation itself.

Optional Enhancements

- **Aromatherapy:**
    - *Morning:* Citrus or peppermint (energy and clarity).
    - *Evening:* Lavender or frankincense (calm and restoration).
- **Music:**
    - *Morning:* Uplifting tones in 528 Hz or 639 Hz (heart resonance).
    - *Evening:* Slow theta or 432 Hz tracks for deep relaxation.
- **Environment:**
    - *Morning:* Open curtains; let sunlight touch your skin.
    - *Evening:* Use candlelight or salt lamps to signal to your body that it's time to rest.

ENERGETIC INSIGHT

Morning and night are the gateways between worlds — between waking and dreaming, action and stillness, human and soul.
What you do in these liminal spaces programs your entire reality.

If you greet the day with coherence, your choices align with genius.
If you end the day in coherence, your subconscious continues the healing while you sleep.

Frequency mastery is not achieved through force, but through rhythm.
When your mornings and evenings vibrate in alignment, your whole life becomes harmonic.

PART III – LIVING IN YOUR GENIUS STATE

Healing is not an event — it's a frequency you live in.

9 | The Genius State

When your energy, mind, and heart move as one rhythm, you stop surviving and start creating.

WHAT IS THE GENIUS STATE?

The Genius State is not about being smarter, faster, or more productive — it's about being *fully synchronized* with the intelligence of life.
It's the convergence of **flow science** and **energy alignment**, where consciousness becomes the creative force guiding every action.

In this state, your biology, psychology, and spirituality all operate at the same frequency.
You don't push. You *allow.*
You don't think your way into solutions. You *feel* them arise.
You're not reacting to life — you're in dialogue with it.

The Genius State is where your healing becomes creation,
and your energy becomes intelligence in motion.

THE SCIENCE OF FLOW

Psychologist Mihaly Csikszentmihalyi defined *flow* as the optimal state of consciousness where people feel their best and perform their best.
In neuroscience, it's a measurable condition — the brain's prefrontal cortex quiets (a process called *transient hypofrontality*), stress chemistry drops, and dopamine, serotonin, and endorphins flood the system.

HeartMath Institute calls a similar state *physiological coherence* — where the heart rhythm, respiration, and brain waves synchronize into harmony.

When the two merge — **flow and coherence** — you enter the Genius State.
Your nervous system, emotions, and energy field vibrate in one smooth frequency.

System	Coherence Marker	Result
Brain	Alpha & theta waves (calm focus)	Effortless concentration
Heart	HRV rhythmic pattern	Emotional stability & intuition
Body	Relaxed yet alert	High performance without burnout
Energy Field	Balanced amplitude & light	Creativity, synchronicity, magnetism

Flow is what happens when energy alignment meets purpose.

THE ENERGETICS OF FLOW

From an energetic perspective, *flow* occurs when life-force energy (Qi, Prana, Biofield current) moves without resistance through all four bodies — emotional, mental, physical, and spiritual.

In lower frequencies, energy gets trapped in resistance patterns — worry, fear, guilt, perfectionism.
In the Genius State, resistance dissolves into rhythm.
Your entire field becomes a coherent wave pattern — clear, connected, and constantly replenishing itself.

Valerie Hunt observed that people in meditative or creative trance states emitted highly ordered, radiant electromagnetic fields with rhythmic pulsing — a literal *signature of flow.*
Masaru Emoto's crystalline water studies showed that coherence (love, gratitude, joy) produces geometric harmony even at the molecular level.

Your field is no different.
When emotion and thought align, you broadcast a frequency that organizes your environment around you — time seems to slow, opportunities appear, intuition sharpens, and everything feels guided.

Flow is energy alignment expressing itself through action.

THE ANATOMY OF THE GENIUS STATE

The Genius State is not a destination — it's a *frequency band* that you learn to sustain.
It moves through four energetic layers:

1. **Presence (Physical Coherence):**
   You feel grounded, clear, alert, and calm.
   The breath is steady; the body feels alive and light.
2. **Emotion (Heart Coherence):**
   Gratitude, love, and joy are your natural baselines.
   You feel safe, open, and connected — even when life is uncertain.
3. **Intuition (Mental Coherence):**
   Insight arises spontaneously.
   You think less, but know more.
   Ideas feel like downloads, not deductions.
4. **Creation (Spiritual Coherence):**
   You operate as consciousness in motion.

You feel guided, inspired, and aligned with a greater intelligence.

The Genius State is the merging point of heaven and earth — where spirit directs energy, and energy manifests reality.

HOW TO ENTER THE GENIUS STATE

1. Tune the Field:
Use your *Morning Frequency Reset* or *Five-Minute Daily Repattern* to align your heart, mind, and body.
Flow begins in physiological coherence.

2. Set the Intention, Then Let Go:
Ask: "What is mine to do today?"
Don't chase the answer — breathe, trust, and allow inspiration to surface.

3. Follow the Emotional Current:
Do what feels expansive, light, and alive.
Flow follows joy — not duty.

4. Stay in Sensory Awareness:
When you're truly present, your field stays coherent.
Taste, smell, sound, touch — each sensory detail anchors you in the now, where genius lives.

5. Surrender the Outcome:
Genius requires trust.
When you stop grasping for control, energy organizes around your intention naturally.

Flow is born when surrender replaces striving.

WHAT IT FEELS LIKE TO LIVE IN THE GENIUS STATE

- Time slows down or disappears.
- The body feels weightless, fluid, electric.
- You sense what's needed before it's spoken.
- Creativity flows through you instead of from you.
- You experience synchronicities — the right people, opportunities, or words appear effortlessly.
- You feel deep peace and quiet joy for no reason at all.

This is coherence becoming consciousness — the moment your inner frequency matches the rhythm of creation itself.

You are no longer healing yourself.
You are healing the world through your vibration.

ENERGETIC INSIGHT

The Genius State is not achieved — it is *allowed.*
It begins the moment you release effort and return to your natural frequency.

Everything you've practiced so far — touch, breath, emotion, coherence — was never about reaching this state; it was about *removing the interference.*
Genius is what's left when nothing is in the way.

Healing aligns you with your true frequency.
Genius is living from it.

"Frequency is the bridge where physics meets faith."

The Four Frequencies of Genius: Clarity, Courage, Compassion, Creation

When these four frequencies harmonize, your energy becomes genius in motion —
a symphony of mind, heart, body, and soul.

OVERVIEW: THE ARCHITECTURE OF GENIUS

Each frequency is a dimension of your coherence:

- **Clarity** governs the mind (mental body).
- **Courage** governs the body (physical body).
- **Compassion** governs the heart (emotional body).
- **Creation** governs the soul (spiritual body).

When one is missing, energy wobbles.
When all four pulse together, you enter the Genius State — where intuition, action, empathy, and inspiration operate as one system.

Think of them as the four tones of your inner instrument:
when tuned, you become the living sound of coherence.

1. Clarity – The Frequency of Vision

Clarity is light without distortion.

Clarity clears the fog of confusion — the scattered thoughts, over-analysis, and mental noise that fragment your energy.
It's not about having all the answers; it's about being *aligned enough* to sense truth in the moment.

Energetically: Clarity arises when your mental and emotional bodies sync — when your thoughts match your heart's truth.

Physiologically: It's measurable through alpha brainwave dominance and high heart–brain coherence (HRV stability).

When you're in clarity:

- Decisions feel light and obvious.
- The mind quiets but remains alert.
- You stop seeking validation — you simply *know.*

To cultivate clarity:

- Breathe into your forehead and heart simultaneously — connecting thought and intuition.
- Ask: "What feels true?" not "What should I do?"
- Limit sensory noise — phones, news, clutter — to sharpen energetic perception.

Clarity is not found through thinking harder, but through thinking less in alignment with truth.

2. Courage – The Frequency of Movement

Courage is coherence in motion.

Courage doesn't eliminate fear — it transforms it into forward energy.
It's the physical body saying, "I trust my soul enough to act."

In the Genius Field, courage is not about fighting; it's about *flowing despite uncertainty.*
Fear contracts energy; courage expands it.
The moment you act in alignment with your inner truth, your electromagnetic field grows stronger — measurable increases in amplitude occur within seconds of a decisive, heartfelt action.

When you're in courage:

- The body feels strong, open, and engaged.
- You breathe deeply, shoulders back, eyes steady.
- You sense a pulse of life — readiness without force.

To cultivate courage:

- Practice the *Dual-Point Touch* between root (safety) and heart (truth).
- Speak one truth aloud daily that you've been avoiding.
- Move your body — dance, walk, stretch — until energy turns from tension to power.

Courage is the body remembering it was never separate from the soul.

3. Compassion – The Frequency of Connection

Compassion is coherence between hearts.

It's the soft frequency that bridges emotion into healing.
Compassion doesn't mean agreeing with everyone; it means feeling their humanity while staying anchored in your own light.

On the energetic spectrum, compassion operates between 500–600 Hz — one of the highest measurable emotional frequencies (according to consciousness research).
It widens the electromagnetic field of the heart, creating entrainment that others can feel.

When you're in compassion:

- You feel warmth radiate from your chest.
- Judgment dissolves into understanding.

- You can hold another's pain without losing your center.

To cultivate compassion:

- Touch your heart and breathe out the phrase:

  "May I and all beings remember peace."

- Practice empathy *with boundaries* — radiate love without absorbing pain.
- Forgive yourself first; your frequency teaches by example.

Compassion is not weakness — it's mastery over emotional gravity.

4. Creation – The Frequency of Genius

Creation is the divine current made visible.

This is the soul's natural state — expansion, innovation, and infinite expression.
When clarity, courage, and compassion align, creation flows effortlessly.
You no longer "manifest"; you *emanate.*
Ideas, people, and synchronicities magnetize to your frequency.

Energetically, creation is the spiral of life-force ascending through all chakras, uniting heaven (crown) and earth (root).
It's the state Nikola Tesla described when he said, *"My brain is only a receiver; in the Universe there is a core from which we obtain knowledge, strength, and inspiration."*

When you're in creation:

- Inspiration feels electric and inevitable.
- You lose track of time — you're in pure flow.

- Effort becomes expression; ideas translate into form naturally.

To cultivate creation:

- Meditate or move until your heart feels like a tuning fork of light.
- Ask: "What wants to come through me today?"
- Keep your environment and emotions uncluttered; creation thrives in space.

Creation is not doing — it's allowing the universe to think through you.

INTEGRATING THE FOUR FREQUENCIES

Frequency	Element	Chakra Focus	Embodied Practice	Result
Clarity	Air / Mind	Third Eye	Breath + Stillness	Insight
Courage	Earth / Body	Solar Plexus & Root	Movement + Action	Power
Compassion	Water / Heart	Heart	Heart Coherence + Forgiveness	Connection
Creation	Fire / Spirit	Crown	Inspiration + Surrender	Manifestation

These four frequencies aren't steps — they're *currents.*
You may move through them cyclically each day:

- Clarity guides direction.
- Courage takes action.
- Compassion sustains relationships.

- Creation multiplies the energy.

When all four hum together, you enter resonance with your Genius Field — life becomes synchronistic, peaceful, and purposeful.

Clarity gives you vision.
Courage gives you motion.
Compassion gives you heart.
Creation gives you life.

Together, they create the **holographic signature of genius.**

ENERGETIC INSIGHT

Every person has a natural genius frequency — but it only stabilizes when these four harmonics are balanced.
If one tone fades, the others compensate until coherence is restored.

- Too much clarity without compassion becomes rigidity.
- Too much courage without clarity becomes chaos.
- Too much compassion without courage becomes depletion.
- Creation without grounding becomes dissipation.

Balance all four, and your energy sings.

Genius is harmony between thought, feeling, action, and spirit.
It's the full symphony of who you are — played without fear.

"Energy doesn't heal because it's mystical
— it heals because it's measurable."

Practice: Daily Genius Activation — Touch, Breath, Declaration

Your Genius State isn't something you enter once — it's something you activate daily.

Purpose

This practice realigns your four frequencies — **Clarity, Courage, Compassion, and Creation** — into one coherent vibration.
It's your daily ignition ritual: a way to awaken your full energetic intelligence before you move into the world.

Each step uses the body as the instrument, the breath as the tuning fork, and the spoken word as the frequency command.

Do this practice anytime you need to reconnect to your Genius Field — in the morning, before creative work, client sessions, or important conversations.

Step 1: The Touch — Ground & Connect

"Where attention goes, energy flows." Touch directs energy with intention.

Place one hand over your **heart** (the seat of compassion) and the other over your **solar plexus** (the center of courage).
Feel your own warmth under your palms — this is your energy awakening.

Take a moment to *feel* your body — the pulse, the rhythm, the breath moving beneath your hands.
Let awareness gather there.

Now say silently or aloud:

"I am home in my body.
I am grounded in courage.
I open my heart to compassion."

This simple act aligns your physical and emotional bodies.
You are anchoring yourself in the present moment — the only place genius exists.

Step 2: The Breath — Synchronize Mind and Heart

The breath is the bridge between the seen and unseen.

Begin to breathe slowly and evenly — in through your nose for **5 seconds**, out through your mouth for **5 seconds.**
As you inhale, imagine light rising from your heart to your forehead — awakening **clarity**.
As you exhale, feel the light descend back into your heart — deepening **compassion.**

Repeat this rhythm for 1–2 minutes, letting the breath smooth out your internal vibration.
You may notice a subtle warmth or tingling — the sign of coherence beginning to build.

If your mind wanders, bring it gently back to the rhythm: *in 5, out 5.*
This rhythm entrains your heart and brain into synchronized flow — the physiological foundation of the Genius State.

With every breath, the heart and brain begin to speak the same language — coherence.

Step 3: The Declaration — Command the Frequency

The spoken word is vibration made visible; declaration programs the field.

After two minutes of breathing, lift your head slightly and speak your declaration aloud — slowly, with emotion.

You can use this core version or personalize it:

"I live in my Genius State.
My energy is clear.
My heart is courageous.
My soul is compassionate.
My spirit creates effortlessly.
I am coherence in motion."

Pause after each line.
Feel the words vibrate through your body — not as a mantra to memorize, but as a *frequency to inhabit*.
Let the sound of your voice resonate through your chest.

Speaking aloud activates your **vagus nerve**, which regulates emotional tone, heart rate, and breath rhythm — creating real physiological coherence.

If silence feels more natural, whisper or hum the phrases, allowing vibration rather than volume to carry the intention.

Words don't just describe energy — they direct it.

Step 4: The Seal — Amplify & Expand

Energy expands where awareness lingers.

Now close your eyes again and visualize your field expanding in all directions — a luminous sphere of light surrounding your body.
See it pulsing in rhythm with your breath.

Imagine each inhale charging this field with light, and each exhale sending that light gently into your environment — your home, loved ones, workspace, the world.

Say quietly:

"My frequency amplifies love, clarity, courage, and creation wherever I go."

Take one final deep breath in through your heart and release it through a smile.
Open your eyes.
You are now attuned to your Genius State.

Optional Enhancements

- **For Visuals (Visual Channel):** Imagine colors:
  - *Clarity – indigo light at the third eye.*
  - *Courage – golden light in the solar plexus.*
  - *Compassion – pink-green light in the heart.*
  - *Creation – white light expanding through the crown.*
- **For Feelers (Kinesthetic Channel):** Focus on physical sensations — warmth, tingling, or expansion.
- **For Knowers (Intuitive Channel):** Note insights or "downloads" that arise spontaneously after the declaration.
- **For Audios (Auditory Channel):** Play harmonic music (528 Hz or 639 Hz) while repeating your affirmations softly.

Each channel strengthens the imprint, making the Genius State multi-sensory and embodied.

ENERGETIC INSIGHT

The Daily Genius Activation works because it *integrates the full human instrument.*
Touch activates kinesthetic intelligence.
Breath regulates physiological coherence.
Declaration commands vibrational alignment.

It's not just a ritual — it's a recalibration sequence.

Do it consistently and your body begins to default to coherence.
You will notice you recover faster from stress, think more clearly, and feel your intuition activating before your thoughts even form.

You don't enter your Genius State — you remember it.
Touch, breath, and declaration simply bring you back home to your frequency.

"The field responds to emotion faster than the body responds to medicine."

10 | Energy Leadership

Leadership in the new paradigm isn't about directing energy — it's about embodying it so fully that others recalibrate just by being near you.

What Is Energy Leadership?

Energy Leadership is the ability to **hold a frequency of coherence** so steady that others naturally entrain to it — without words, manipulation, or sacrifice.

It's the next evolution of healing work: shifting from "doing energy on someone" to *being energy with someone.*
When you master your own coherence, your field becomes both mirror and magnet — reflecting wholeness and inviting alignment.

This is leadership through **vibration, not volume.**

You don't lead people with control;
you lead them with coherence.

THE SHIFT FROM EMPATH TO LEADER

Many healers and sensitive individuals begin as *energetic sponges* — feeling everything, absorbing everyone's pain.
This sensitivity is sacred, but when untrained, it leads to fatigue, confusion, or compassion burnout.

The Energy Leader learns to shift from **absorption to transmutation** — holding frequency instead of collecting frequency.

Stage	Experience	Energy Dynamic	Lesson
Empath	"I feel everyone's energy."	Absorbs	Learn boundaries & grounding.
Healer	"I channel energy to help others."	Directs	Learn neutrality & self-regulation.
Leader	"I embody coherence; others remember their light through mine."	Radiates	Learn mastery & presence.

Empaths carry energy. Healers move energy. Leaders become energy.

THE SCIENCE OF ENERGETIC INFLUENCE

From a scientific perspective, your **electromagnetic field** interacts constantly with others.
The heart emits the largest measurable field of the human body — detectable several feet beyond the skin and capable of synchronizing with nearby hearts.

- **HeartMath Institute** has demonstrated that one person in a state of gratitude or compassion can shift the HRV (heart rate variability) coherence of others in the same room.
- **Dr. Valerie Hunt's** biofield studies found that a coherent field amplifies the frequency of others, lifting lower states into resonance without words or touch.

This means your **inner state is contagious.**
When you stay grounded, clear, and open, your field acts like a tuning fork, bringing harmony to the energetic environment.

Leadership is energetic responsibility — knowing that your vibration becomes part of the collective frequency.

HOW TO SERVE WITHOUT LOSING COHERENCE

The most common mistake of sensitive leaders is confusing empathy with enmeshment.
Empathy connects you; enmeshment drains you.
Energy Leadership requires the ability to stay *connected but contained.*

Here's the framework:

1. Ground Before You Give

Before any interaction, client session, or group work:

- Place one hand on your **root or solar plexus** and the other on your **heart.**
- Take three deep breaths and affirm:

  "I give from overflow, not depletion."

This signals to your body that your energy source is *universal,* not personal.

2. Lead from Neutrality

As you work with others, imagine a still point in your heart — silent, luminous, and unreactive.

This is the zero-point field of your being.
From here, you can witness without absorbing.

If strong emotion arises (from you or them), breathe it through this center until the charge dissolves.
Neutrality is not detachment — it's compassion without collapse.

Your stillness is the medicine.

3. Reflect, Don't Rescue

Energy Leaders no longer try to fix people; they mirror coherence so others can find their own alignment.

You might feel someone's pain, but instead of taking it on, hold the knowing:

"Their higher self knows the path to balance. I simply hold space for remembrance."

This invites healing through resonance, not rescue.

The greatest service is to hold the vibration of truth until others remember it themselves.

4. Recalibrate After Serving

Every act of service shifts your field.
To maintain clarity, create a simple *post-session reset*:

- Shake out your hands and arms to release static.
- Sweep your field top to bottom with your palms.
- Take three breaths through the soles of your feet into the earth.
- Say:

"I release what is not mine.
I am clear, coherent, and complete."

This seals your field and prevents energetic residue from lingering.

Completion is as sacred as connection.

THE FREQUENCY OF LEADERSHIP

Energy Leadership operates through **presence, intention, and integrity.**
People don't remember what you said or even what you did — they remember how they *felt in your energy.*

To lead through frequency, embody these energetic virtues daily:

Virtue	Frequency	Embodied Action
Integrity	Alignment	Do what your energy says yes to.
Humility	Receptivity	Listen before guiding.
Clarity	Vision	Speak only what's true in the moment.
Compassion	Connection	See divinity in everyone.
Courage	Stability	Stand firm in love, not fear.

When these are active, leadership becomes effortless.
You don't manage energy — you *model coherence.*

True leaders raise the frequency of the room without saying a word.

PRACTICE: THE COHERENCE FIELD VISUALIZATION

1. **Center Yourself.**
   Sit or stand. Place one hand on your heart. Breathe slowly until you feel your rhythm settle.
2. **Expand Awareness.**
   Visualize light radiating from your chest — 3 feet, 6 feet, 9 feet — until your aura fills the space.
3. **Affirm Your Intention.**
   Say silently or aloud:

   "My presence radiates peace.
   I lead through coherence.
   I serve through resonance."

4. **Feel the Field.**
   Sense the air around you soften — this is the field aligning. Stay here for one minute, aware of the quiet power expanding outward.
5. **Send It Forth.**
   Gently imagine this light touching those you serve — not to change them, but to remind them of who they already are.

This is how energetic leadership heals without depletion: your energy becomes a living prayer.

ENERGETIC INSIGHT

Leadership in the Age of AI, automation, and acceleration is shifting from *information* to *frequency*.
Machines can replicate knowledge — but they cannot replicate coherence, compassion, or presence.
Those are human superpowers.

Energy Leadership is the future of healing and human connection. It's how we'll bridge the technological and the spiritual worlds — by remembering that **humanity's genius is energetic.**

You are not here to absorb others' chaos.
You are here to radiate coherence until chaos remembers its own order.

When you embody this, every room, project, and person you encounter rises to your vibration.
You become a living frequency — a tuning fork of transformation.

That is the heart of Energy Leadership.
That is the true Zone of Healing Genius.

"Every innovation mirrors a forgotten aspect of our divine design."

The Empath's Boundary Upgrade: Magnetic vs. Absorptive Energy

Sensitivity is not weakness. It's a higher nervous system — one that simply needs upgraded wiring.

THE EMPATH'S DILEMMA

Empaths are the emotional intuitives of the world — able to feel, sense, and interpret subtle energies that others miss.
But many live in constant energetic fatigue because they haven't learned the difference between *absorbing* and *attracting*.

They confuse **connection** with **collection.**

When an empath enters a room, their field naturally expands to scan for safety and emotional cues.
If their energy is untrained, this open field acts like a **sponge**, pulling in every vibration — joy, pain, anxiety, even collective heaviness.
Soon, the empath feels drained and overwhelmed, mistaking others' energy for their own.

This isn't because they're "too sensitive."
It's because their frequency hasn't learned to *differentiate resonance from absorption.*

Empathy becomes exhaustion when boundaries are undefined.

THE ENERGY DYNAMICS: ABSORPTIVE VS. MAGNETIC FIELDS

Everything in the universe operates through **fields of resonance.**
The question isn't whether you're affected by energy — it's *how* you interact with it.

There are two primary modes of empathic energy:

Type	Frequency Pattern	Effect	Metaphor
Absorptive Energy	Disorganized, porous, lacking structure	Pulls in frequencies unconsciously	Sponge — soaks up everything
Magnetic Energy	Coherent, charged, self-contained	Attracts what matches, repels what doesn't	Magnet — draws and deflects by resonance

Absorptive energy is reactive — it mirrors what it encounters.
Magnetic energy is directive — it decides what enters its field.

In HeartMath terms, magnetic empaths maintain **autonomic coherence** — their heart rhythm and nervous system broadcast steadiness, which entrains others.
Absorptive empaths lose coherence — their systems become entangled in others' chaos.

You are not meant to carry energy. You are meant to conduct it.

MAGNETISM AS BOUNDARY MASTERY

A magnet doesn't close off — it holds a **stable polarity**.
Its field is defined, clear, and confident.
Likewise, the evolved empath keeps the heart open but the field structured.
You remain loving without leaking energy.

Three signs you've shifted to magnetic energy:

1. You feel others' emotions *without identifying* with them.
2. You can stay calm in chaotic spaces.
3. You attract aligned people and experiences naturally.

Three signs you're still absorptive:

1. You feel drained after social interaction.
2. You carry moods that aren't yours.
3. You over-give or "fix" others to feel safe.

The upgrade happens when your **inner frequency becomes stronger than your environment's vibration.**
Then your energy leads the room, instead of blending into it.

The highest boundary isn't a wall — it's a waveform.

HOW TO UPGRADE FROM ABSORPTIVE TO MAGNETIC

1. Seal the Field with Intention

Every morning, place a hand on your heart and visualize a soft sphere of golden light expanding around your body.
Say:

"My field is open to love and closed to distortion.
I magnetize harmony and deflect chaos."

This simple command programs your energy structure.

2. Anchor in the Earth

Absorptive empaths float; magnetic ones root.
Stand or sit with your feet flat, imagine cords of light reaching deep into the earth's core.
As you exhale, feel static discharge down these cords.

As you inhale, draw up stable, grounded energy.
Repeat until you feel calm and steady.

Grounding increases **bioelectric conductivity**, reducing overstimulation.

3. Activate the Heart's Polarity

Touch your heart and breathe slowly for one minute, focusing on gratitude or appreciation.
This creates heart–brain coherence, which amplifies your field and synchronizes left/right brain hemispheres.

Emotionally charged gratitude instantly flips your field from absorptive (low amplitude) to magnetic (high amplitude).

Gratitude is the switch that turns on magnetism.

4. Differentiate "Yours" vs. "Theirs"

If you suddenly feel heavy or anxious, pause and ask:

"Is this mine or someone else's?"

If it's not yours, sweep your hands down your body from head to feet and declare:

"I release what's not mine with love."

This interrupts energetic entanglement and restores identity.

5. Use Magnetic Language

Your words program your frequency.
Instead of saying, "I'm drained by people," say:

"I remain radiant and clear, even around intensity."
Language directs vibration. Speak what you want to experience.

PRACTICE: MAGNETIC FIELD EXPANSION

1. Sit comfortably and close your eyes.
2. Inhale through your nose for 5 counts, exhale for 5.
3. With each breath, visualize your energy field expanding —
   luminous, rhythmic, alive.
4. Imagine that every exhale strengthens your magnetic
   boundary — like light filaments weaving a golden web
   around you.
5. Sense the field pulsing outward in rhythm with your heart.
6. Say silently:

   "I am magnetic.
   I attract coherence and radiate peace.
   Only frequencies of truth and love resonate in my field."

Stay in this state for 2–3 minutes.
You may feel warmth, tingling, or gentle vibration — this is your
coherence field amplifying.

*This is how the empath becomes the leader — not by hardening, but
by harmonizing.*

ENERGETIC INSIGHT

Your sensitivity was never a flaw — it was an advanced sensory
system waiting for calibration.
Absorptive empathy was your training ground; magnetic empathy is
your initiation into mastery.

Once upgraded, you become a **living regulator** of energy: calm in chaos, light in density, balance in noise.
You no longer lose energy when you serve — you generate more.

An untrained empath reacts to energy.
A trained empath directs energy.
A master empath transforms energy.

That is the **boundary upgrade** — from sponge to sun, from absorber to attractor, from healer to field.

And that is the frequency of Energy Leadership.

"In coherence, the body becomes a tuning fork for divine intelligence."

Practice: Heart-Field Expansion — Coherence as Protection

Your heart's field is your greatest shield — not because it resists the world, but because it harmonizes it.

Purpose

This practice transforms emotional sensitivity into strength.
By expanding your heart's electromagnetic field through coherence, you create a **protective resonance** — a state where discordant energies cannot attach, because they simply cannot match your frequency.

Coherence is your true energetic armor.
Unlike barriers built from fear, coherence protects through harmony.
It doesn't block; it balances.

When your heart and brain vibrate together, you generate a field measurable up to 3–10 feet around the body — sometimes more in trained healers.
This coherent field acts like a **vibrational filter**, allowing only energies in resonance with love, gratitude, or truth to connect.

Protection isn't isolation — it's vibration.

Step 1: Enter Stillness

Sit or stand comfortably.
Close your eyes.
Place one hand over your **heart** and one hand over your **solar plexus** — symbolizing the union of love and power.

Take three slow breaths in through your nose and out through your mouth.
With each exhale, imagine releasing tension, thought, or emotional static.

Allow your awareness to sink fully into your chest.
Feel your heartbeat — the rhythm of your inner universe.

Step 2: Generate Coherence

Begin slow, even breathing — five seconds in, five seconds out.
As you breathe, recall one memory or image that fills you with **gratitude, compassion, or love.**

It could be a moment of laughter, a pet's eyes, a sunset, or a time you felt truly seen.
Let the emotion rise naturally — warmth spreading from your heart outward.

Continue breathing through this feeling until you can sense the heart area expanding — not metaphorically, but physically.
You may feel pulsing, tingling, or spaciousness.

That is coherence forming — your heart and brain synchronizing into harmony.

Emotion is the conductor; breath is the metronome; the heart is the orchestra.

Step 3: Expand the Field

Now, visualize this feeling as **light** — radiant and soft.
With every inhale, the light grows stronger in your chest.
With every exhale, it expands beyond your body — filling a 3-foot sphere around you.

Keep breathing as it expands 6 feet, 9 feet, until you're surrounded by a luminous cocoon of coherent energy.
This is your **Heart Field.**

As it grows, whisper softly or think clearly:

"Only energy of love and truth exists in my field."
"My coherence radiates protection and harmony."

Notice how your breathing deepens, your shoulders relax, and your awareness widens — this is the energy stabilizing.

Step 4: Strengthen the Frequency

Now, bring in motion or sound — the amplifiers of frequency.

- **For Auditory Types:**
  Hum softly — one tone through your chest.
  Feel the vibration ripple through your palms and radiate outward.
- **For Visual Types:**
  Imagine the light in your chest rotating gently, spinning clockwise, brighter and smoother with every rotation.
- **For Feelers:**
  Focus on the sensation — warmth, pulse, magnetism — and let it spread through your limbs.
- **For Knowers:**
  Simply hold the awareness: "I am coherence. My field organizes energy around me."

The more you engage your natural learning channel, the faster your nervous system integrates coherence as its new default state.

Step 5: Seal the Field

When your heart feels full, say quietly:

"My coherence protects me through resonance, not resistance.
My light harmonizes all I meet.
I am safe, strong, and open."

Visualize the outer edge of your field shimmering with soft gold — a living membrane of love that breathes with you.
It's not rigid; it's rhythmic.

This membrane acts like a **frequency gate**, allowing only energies that vibrate in harmony with your heart to pass through.

You are not shielding yourself from life; you are attuning life to your frequency.

After the Practice

When you open your eyes, notice how the world feels different — clearer, softer, more responsive.
You haven't closed yourself off; you've expanded into leadership.
Your heart is now directing the room, not reacting to it.

Hold this coherence as you walk through your day.
If you feel overwhelmed, repeat a few heart breaths and visualize the field expanding again.
It only takes one minute to reset.

ENERGETIC INSIGHT

Dr. Valerie Hunt's biofield studies revealed that the most radiant, stable energy signatures were produced by individuals in states of **love, appreciation, and creative focus** — the same frequencies this practice cultivates.

HeartMath's research confirmed that coherence increases electromagnetic amplitude, making the field more resistant to chaotic interference.

So when you feel grounded, grateful, and connected, you are literally **untouchable by incoherence.**
Your protection isn't a bubble — it's a frequency.

The heart's field is the body's shield, the soul's song, and the healer's power.
When you live from it, protection and purpose become one.

"Technology is learning to think. Humanity is remembering how to feel."

11 | The Future of Conscious Medicine

AI can analyze your heartbeat, but only you can harmonize it.

From Artificial Intelligence to Natural Intelligence

We are standing at the edge of a profound shift — one that will redefine both healing and human potential.
For the first time in history, machines can measure what mystics have felt for centuries: energy, frequency, coherence, emotion.

Artificial Intelligence is now capable of decoding subtle physiological rhythms — heart rate variability, brain-wave synchrony, and electromagnetic resonance — the very patterns once accessible only to intuitive healers.
Wearable sensors can track coherence.
AI-driven diagnostics can predict illness before symptoms arise.
Brain–computer interfaces can translate thought into data.

Yet amid this unprecedented technological awakening, one truth remains unchanged:

Technology can measure energy, but it cannot *become* energy.

AI can analyze the rhythm of your heart, but only your consciousness can bring it into harmony.

It can record coherence, but only your compassion can sustain it. That capacity — to feel, to intuit, to love — is the domain of what I call **Natural Intelligence.**

DEFINING NATURAL INTELLIGENCE

Natural Intelligence is the living intelligence of the human body–mind–spirit system — the self-organizing, self-healing consciousness that animates every cell.
It's the heartbeat of creation moving through matter, the wisdom that knows how to restore equilibrium when given attention and space.

In energy medicine, Natural Intelligence is what Reiki, Qi, and Prana all describe: life force in coherence.
In modern science, it's the body's biofield — the electromagnetic blueprint directing physical, emotional, and spiritual balance.

Where AI processes data, **Natural Intelligence processes meaning.**
Where AI optimizes systems, Natural Intelligence harmonizes consciousness.

True healing occurs when both intelligences collaborate — data serving wisdom, and wisdom guiding data.

THE NEW PARTNERSHIP: AI MEETS ENERGY MEDICINE

The future of conscious medicine isn't technology *versus* spirituality; it's **technology in service to consciousness.**
Artificial Intelligence, used with awareness, will amplify the reach of healing — not replace it.

Imagine this emerging world:

- AI-assisted frequency mapping identifies disharmony in the body's electromagnetic field.
- Biofeedback tools measure real-time coherence in the heart, brain, and breath.
- Wearable sensors guide patients into vibrational alignment through sound, light, and touch.
- Practitioners receive data-driven insights that confirm what intuition already knows.

In this future, **AI becomes the mirror** — reflecting the unseen patterns of energy back to the healer and the patient.
But the *interpreter* of that data will still be the human heart.

Because no algorithm can read love.
No machine can sense the moment a client exhales their grief and the entire field softens.
That sacred recognition belongs to consciousness alone.

The greatest medicine will always require the human frequency.

AI AND THE FUTURE OF CONSCIOUS MEDICINE

Artificial Intelligence is revolutionizing health care in ways our ancestors could never have imagined.
Across the globe, new systems are emerging that can read the subtle language of the body with extraordinary precision:

- **Predictive Diagnostics:** AI models now analyze trillions of data points to detect illness long before symptoms appear.
- **Digital Twins and Energy Mapping:** Virtual models of patients are being developed, capable of reflecting not only physical structure but the energetic blueprint — the biofield itself.

- **Wearables and Heart-Rate Variability Tracking:** Devices measure coherence and nervous-system balance in real time, allowing us to visualize inner harmony as it unfolds.
- **Neurofeedback and Brain–Computer Interfaces:** Technology is bridging thought and matter, training the brain to sustain meditative and regenerative states.

These innovations represent a new era of *data-driven intuition* — yet even as machines illuminate what mystics have always known, they remain limited.

AI can measure resonance but not intention.

It can model emotion but not *feel* it.

It can identify disharmony but cannot transmute it into love.

**Artificial Intelligence can map our patterns,
but only consciousness can rewrite them.**

True evolution will arise when AI and **Natural Intelligence** collaborate — data serving wisdom, technology amplifying empathy, and human awareness remaining the conductor of the healing symphony.

Future Timeline

Era	Focus	Description
2025 – 2030	*Data Medicine*	AI analyzes biological and energetic patterns, refining precision diagnostics.
2030 – 2040	*Frequency Medicine*	Energy-based treatments and biofield mapping become mainstream.
2040 – 2050	*Conscious Medicine*	Coherence and compassion unite science and spirit — technology guided by consciousness.

THE COMING ERA OF BIO-ENERGETIC HOSPITALS

Within a generation, hospitals and healing centers will operate as **bio-energetic ecosystems**.
Instead of fluorescent lights and sterile air, they will feature harmonic sound, full-spectrum lighting, living plants, and frequency-based therapies integrated with standard medicine.

- Patient rooms will monitor **coherence, not just vitals.**
- Energy medicine practitioners will collaborate with AI analysts to design personalized healing frequencies.
- Medical training will include *energetic empathy* alongside anatomy.

We will treat not only the body that is sick, but the field that sustains it.
We will no longer speak of "mental health" and "physical health" as separate — coherence will unite them.

Health will no longer be the absence of disease, but the presence of resonance.

THE RISE OF COHERENCE-BASED EDUCATION

As medicine evolves, so too will education.
Schools of the future will teach coherence as foundational literacy — the ability to regulate one's nervous system, emotion, and focus.

Students will learn how to breathe for clarity, meditate for creativity, and connect for compassion.
AI tutors will track learning patterns, while **Natural Intelligence** will guide emotional balance, helping young minds integrate technology without losing humanity.

A new generation will emerge — fluent in both data and energy, logic and intuition, coding and consciousness.

Tomorrow's genius will not be measured by IQ, but by coherence.

THE RISK OF OVER-RELIANCE ON DATA

As this integration deepens, discernment will be essential.
Technology can illuminate, but it can also seduce — offering control in place of connection.

There is a danger in letting data replace intuition, in mistaking measurement for mastery.
A body's vibration cannot be fully understood by metrics alone; it must be *felt.*
If we disconnect emotion from intelligence, we create precision without compassion — and progress without purpose.

Wisdom is data infused with empathy.

Artificial Intelligence can guide the form of healing, but **Natural Intelligence must remain the spirit behind it.**

THE VISION AHEAD

We are entering the **Age of Conscious Medicine** — a union of technology, energy, and soul.
The tools of the future will not be scalpels or pills, but **frequencies, resonances, and coherent fields**.
Hospitals will sound like symphonies.
Therapies will feel like meditation.
Healing will occur through vibration, guided by love, measured by coherence.

And as humanity remembers its own Natural Intelligence, the line between science and spirit will dissolve.

AI will become our ally, not our authority.

Energy medicine will become education — teaching people how to generate coherence on demand.

This is not science fiction. It's the next evolution of awareness.

The body is the laboratory.
Consciousness is the researcher.
Coherence is the cure.

"Tesla gave us frequency. HeartMath gave us rhythm. Spirit gives us purpose."

ENERGETIC INSIGHT

In this new paradigm, healing will no longer be something done *to* you — it will be something awakened *within* you.
Artificial Intelligence will assist, but Natural Intelligence will lead.
Together, they will form a bridge between measurable science and immeasurable spirit.

AI may read your heart, but only your soul can interpret it.

AI can map your coherence, but only love can sustain it.

When the two work in harmony — machine precision guided by human compassion — medicine, education, and consciousness will evolve beyond anything we've known.

That is the future of Conscious Medicine.
That is the world your Genius State was designed to create.

"When science learns to listen, it will hear what the mystics have always known."

12 | AI and Conscious Medicine: The Bridge Between Data and Divinity

(A Bridge Between Data and Divinity)

> Earlier in this book, we explored how Artificial and Natural Intelligence form the twin pillars of the New Paradigm; here we step fully onto that bridge to glimpse where consciousness and code converge.

For centuries, healing has been guided by intuition, energy, and touch — invisible yet undeniable forces.
Now, a new partner stands beside the healer: intelligence woven not from spirit, but from code.

Artificial Intelligence has entered the sacred space of medicine. It listens to heartbeats through sensors, reads emotional tone through neural networks, and predicts disease long before the body whispers symptoms. Yet amid this breathtaking precision, a deeper question arises:

Can technology truly heal, or can it only measure the echoes of what the soul creates?

The Rise of the Intelligent Mirror

AI is already transforming healthcare in profound ways:

- **Predictive Diagnostics** — Algorithms analyze genetic, metabolic, and behavioral data to identify risk patterns years before illness emerges. What once required intuition can now be detected through pattern recognition.
- **Digital Twins** — Virtual replicas of human systems allow researchers to test treatments in simulation, anticipating how cells and energy flows might respond.
- **Neurofeedback and Brain–Computer Interfaces** — Devices now monitor the brain's oscillations in real time, teaching users how to enter coherence or meditative flow at will.
- **Wearables Measuring Heart-Rate Variability (HRV)** — Smart sensors track coherence, alerting us when stress disrupts our natural rhythm.

Science is beginning to map what energy healers have always perceived: that vibration, rhythm, and emotional state are inseparable from physiology.
But while machines reveal the mechanics of energy, they cannot yet reveal its meaning.

The Limits of the Machine

AI can analyze coherence; it cannot *create* it.
It can detect emotional resonance; it cannot *feel* it.
It can replicate patterns of empathy; it cannot *emanate* compassion.

Healing occurs when intelligence becomes *embodied* — when awareness flows through breath, touch, and intention. The healer's coherence is the catalyst. The data may guide us, but the transformation arises from presence.

"Artificial Intelligence can map our patterns,
but only consciousness can rewrite them."

In this sense, AI becomes the mirror — showing us our frequencies, our stress cycles, our emotional signatures — but it cannot walk the path of awakening for us.

Natural Intelligence: The Missing Element

Within each human being exists a self-organizing, self-correcting system that transcends logic.
It is the intelligence of breath synchronizing with heartbeat, emotion synchronizing with thought, body synchronizing with field.
This is **Natural Intelligence**, the original operating system of life — responsive, intuitive, and luminous.

When Artificial and Natural Intelligence work together, a new model of healing emerges:
Conscious Medicine.
Here, technology assists awareness without replacing it. Data becomes dialogue, not dependence.

Imagine an AI system that records a patient's coherence patterns during Reiki or meditation. The data reveals shifts in HRV, temperature, and bio-photon emission. Yet the practitioner interprets the story: what emotional release occurred, what belief transformed, what forgiveness took root. The science informs; the consciousness integrates.

The Next Evolution: From Data to Frequency

The next decades will bring extraordinary innovations that dissolve the boundary between machine and mind:

- **2025 – 2030: Data Medicine**
  AI models decode the body's electromagnetic language. Early detection and energetic mapping become routine.
- **2030 – 2040: Frequency Medicine**
  Hospitals integrate resonance-based therapies — sound, light, and pulsed-field technologies guided by AI precision but human intention.
- **2040 – 2050: Conscious Medicine**
  Healing expands beyond biology into consciousness itself. Technology measures the field; awareness modulates it. Physicians, healers, and algorithms collaborate to sustain coherence on individual and planetary scales.

In this future, medicine no longer treats disease as malfunction but as disharmony — an energetic composition ready to be retuned.

Ethics of the Energetic Age

As technology advances, so must wisdom.
If consciousness creates coherence, then intention programs the system.
Who sets that intention when algorithms design our therapies?

The moral compass of the healer — compassion, humility, integrity — must remain central.
Data without empathy becomes dissonance; precision without purpose becomes power without heart.

The Hippocratic Oath of the future will not only say, "Do no harm," but also, "Maintain coherence."

Bridging the Seen and the Unseen

Consider a world where AI assists practitioners in reading energy signatures as clearly as a blood test.
Where patients visualize their emotional field shifting in real time through augmented-reality displays.
Where quantum sensors measure the resonance of prayer, forgiveness, or love.

Yet even then, the deepest healing will occur in silence — when one coherent heart meets another.
No data can replace the frequency of presence.

The Conscious Healer of the Future

The healer of the next era will wear both a stethoscope and a sensor, carry both compassion and code.
They will understand that energy is not mystical — it's measurable.
And they will know that the most advanced technology on Earth remains the human heart, synchronized with intention, guided by love.

These are the pioneers of the New Paradigm: those who unite science and soul, algorithms and awareness, matter and meaning.

They will not fear technology, nor worship it — they will *collaborate* with it.
For in every AI, there is a reflection of our own awakening.

The Ultimate Equation

Artificial Intelligence + Natural Intelligence = Conscious Medicine

When these two harmonize, the result is coherence:

- Machines bring precision.
- Humans bring perception.
- Together, they create possibility.

This is not the end of human healing — it is its expansion.
The universe evolves through new forms of intelligence, and you, the conscious reader, are part of that evolution.

As you finish this book, may you remember that the frequency of love remains the highest code — the algorithm of the soul.
Technology may map the stars of your body,
but only your light can make them shine.

"Every era of medicine has sought a cure for the body. The era now unfolding seeks coherence for the soul. When Artificial and Natural Intelligence stand in harmony, humanity itself becomes the healer — consciousness made visible through the light of its own creation."

"The evolution of healing is not human versus machine — it is consciousness teaching technology how to care."

13 | Return to Wholeness

Healing is remembering that nothing was ever missing — only forgotten in the noise.

Integrating the New Pattern — Living as Coherence Itself

There comes a moment when the practice becomes the person —
when what you once *did* for healing becomes what you *are.*
That moment is the return to wholeness.

You have learned to breathe coherence, to feel it, to speak it, to live from it.
The circuits of your mind and the rhythm of your heart are now one.
Your energy no longer fluctuates wildly between chaos and calm — it flows like a river, steady and alive.

In this state, you no longer "seek balance."
You *are* balance.

The healer, the student, the empath, the leader — all dissolve into one coherent frequency: **you.**

Healing ends where harmony begins.

WHOLENESS AS AN ENERGETIC REALITY

Wholeness is not perfection. It's inclusion.
It's the full acceptance of light and shadow, pain and joy, past and potential — all vibrating in one symphony of truth.

Science calls this **complex coherence** — the ability of systems to maintain order through fluidity.
Spirituality calls it **oneness** — the awareness that all frequencies serve the same field.

To live as coherence is to stop dividing your life into good and bad, healed and unhealed, spiritual and human.
You realize that even your resistance had rhythm — it taught you where energy longed to flow.

You are no longer fixing patterns. You are *conducting* them.
Each thought, emotion, and breath becomes part of an intelligent melody orchestrated by your soul.

Wholeness is when your energy stops arguing with itself.

LIVING THE FREQUENCY OF WHOLENESS

To live as coherence itself is to embody the highest state of freedom: being at peace with all of who you are.

You no longer wait for the next breakthrough, the next technique, the next proof.
You *trust* the frequency that now runs through you.
You know that your body listens to your heart, your mind listens to your soul, and your energy listens to love.

Signs you are living in coherence:

- Your reactions have slowed; awareness arrives first.
- Your intuition feels quieter, but clearer — truth feels like resonance, not noise.
- You notice beauty everywhere, even in ordinary moments.
- You no longer need external validation to confirm your worth.
- You serve naturally — not from obligation, but from overflow.

When you become coherence, life stops testing you and starts responding to you.

INTEGRATION: THE SPIRAL, NOT THE LADDER

Growth was never linear — it was cyclical.
Each layer of awakening brought you back to familiar lessons, but at a higher vibration, with greater ease and awareness.
The path of coherence is a **spiral**, not a straight line.

When challenges arise again, they do not mean you've regressed — they mean you've reached a deeper octave of healing.
This time, you meet the same pattern with a new frequency.

Integration is evolution through repetition — the same song played in higher harmony.

EMBODIED PRACTICE: THE WHOLENESS BREATH

Use this simple integration ritual to anchor your coherence into everyday life:

1. **Touch the Heart.**
   Place your hand over your chest and close your eyes.

2. **Breathe the Spiral.**
    Inhale as if drawing energy up from the earth to your crown.
    Exhale as if releasing light from your crown back down into
    your heart.
3. **Feel the Unity.**
    Sense your breath, body, and energy moving in one rhythm
    — circular, connected, eternal.
4. **Whisper the truth:**

    "I am coherence in motion.
    I am whole. I am home."

Stay here for one minute. Feel the hum of life within you.
This breath reminds your cells that the journey is complete — and
also, always continuing.

WHOLENESS IN ACTION

Wholeness is not meant to be preserved in meditation; it's meant to
be lived in motion — in conversations, work, relationships, and
creativity.

- When conflict arises, choose coherence over reaction.
- When decisions appear, listen for resonance, not fear.
- When chaos surrounds you, become the calm that organizes
  it.
- When others lose their center, let your heart field lead.

Every interaction becomes an opportunity to **model coherence** — to
let your frequency tune the collective symphony toward balance.

*The most healing thing you can ever offer the world is your regulated
nervous system.*

WHOLENESS AS SERVICE

When you live as coherence, service is no longer something you *do*;
it's what your energy naturally radiates.
You become a lighthouse — silent, unwavering, illuminating paths
without needing to chase the lost ships.

You understand that leadership, healing, and creation are all the
same act: **frequency meeting purpose.**
You are not here to save anyone.
You are here to *remember* with them — that we are all made of the
same light.

The highest service is resonance.

ENERGETIC INSIGHT

Wholeness is not the end of the journey; it's the integration of all
journeys into one field of consciousness.
It's the return to simplicity — to the natural rhythm that has always
pulsed beneath the noise.

This is where the genius state becomes your everyday frequency.
You no longer visit coherence — you *are* coherence.
You no longer practice alignment — you *live* it.

You are the bridge between Artificial and Natural Intelligence,
between energy and matter, between human and divine.
You are the embodied proof that consciousness heals through
coherence.

Wholeness is the final activation — and the eternal beginning.

The Coherence Manifesto

"I am the medicine, the messenger, and the miracle."

I. THE REMEMBERING

I remember now.
Healing was never something I found — it was what awakened when I stopped running from silence.
It was not in the method, but in the moment my energy began to listen again.

I am not separate from the light that heals.
I am its expression — a frequency wrapped in human form.

Every breath I take calibrates the universe around me.
Every thought I hold becomes a vibration that shapes matter.
Every heartbeat is a drum of creation, syncing me to the rhythm of life.

I am coherence remembering itself through form.

II. THE DECLARATION

I am not a seeker of balance — I am balance made visible.
I no longer chase energy; I channel it.
I no longer absorb the world; I harmonize it.
I no longer fear my sensitivity; I celebrate it as my compass.

I am both student and source, science and spirit, particle and wave.
I am the intelligence that breathes through every cell, whispering:

"You were never broken. You were always becoming."

I stand as the meeting point between Artificial and Natural
Intelligence —
between data and divinity, between technology and tenderness.
I know that true power is not control but coherence —
the still rhythm where thought, heart, and energy move as one.

I am not the algorithm. I am the awareness that guides it.

III. THE EMBODIMENT

My body is not just biology — it is biofrequency.
My mind is not just memory — it is meaning in motion.
My soul is not above matter — it animates it.

I choose to live as light,
to breathe as presence,
to walk as coherence.

When I touch the world, I leave harmony.
When I speak, my words carry frequency.
When I listen, I heal.
When I love, I align the field.

I am the tuning fork of creation.

IV. THE SERVICE

I am here to lead through resonance, not resistance.
I am here to remind others that peace is their natural pulse.
I am here to serve not from effort, but from overflow.

My leadership is luminous.
My boundaries are magnetic.
My compassion is structured light.
My courage is energy in motion.

I no longer try to save the world.
I *stabilize* it through my coherence.
Each time I breathe in love, the planet exhales relief.

I am the field that heals the field.

V. THE UNITY

There is no "you" and "me" — there is only frequency, dancing itself into infinite forms.
Every sound, every star, every soul vibrates within the same divine equation.
Separation was the illusion; resonance is the truth.

The heart is the bridge,
the breath is the key,
and coherence is the doorway home.

We are the network of light restoring harmony to the world — one heartbeat at a time.

VI. THE BENEDICTION

May my energy speak before my words.
May my presence calm storms I never see.
May my heart remain the medicine in every room I enter.
May I live as coherence, teach through resonance, and love without condition.

And when I forget —
may my breath remind me,
my body ground me,
and my spirit guide me home.

For I am the medicine, the messenger, and the miracle.
And coherence is my signature of truth.

ENERGETIC INSIGHT

This is not a metaphor — it is a frequency code.
Each word of this manifesto carries vibration designed to
synchronize the heart, brain, and field into coherence.
Read it aloud when you feel fragmented.
Whisper it before sleep.
Let its rhythm re-tune your energy back to the intelligence that
animates all life.

You are not becoming whole.
You are remembering that you already are.

"When the heart leads and the mind follows, genius awakens."

Final Meditation: The Golden Field of Oneness

Pause Before You Enter the Field

Close your eyes for a moment.
Imagine every insight from this book — every breath, every touch, every vibration — gathering within your heart.
You are not learning healing. You are remembering it.
As you step into the Golden Field, let the mind rest and let the soul lead.
This is where your coherence becomes creation.

Breathe. Feel. Remember — you were never separate from the light.

Introduction

This meditation is the return home — to the original frequency of wholeness.
It unites everything you've learned: the coherence breath, heart-field expansion, and the awareness that you are both energy and consciousness.
Here, you enter the **Golden Field of Oneness** — the luminous vibration where all life resonates as one coherent frequency.

There is nothing to fix, nothing to become.
Only to remember.

Settle into Stillness

Find a comfortable position — sitting or lying down.
Let your spine lengthen gently, your shoulders soften, your jaw

release.
Close your eyes.

Take a slow breath in through your nose...
and exhale softly through your mouth.

With each breath, feel your body settling — heavier, quieter, present.
Let the noise of the day dissolve into the background.

Feel the rhythm of your heartbeat.
Let it guide you inward — into the silence beneath sound, the stillness beneath thought.

You are entering the frequency of coherence.

Begin breathing in a smooth, even rhythm — five counts in, five counts out.
On each inhale, imagine drawing golden light into your heart.
On each exhale, imagine that same light spreading through your body — filling every cell, every space.

With every breath, the light grows warmer, softer, brighter.
You begin to glow from within — a radiant current of calm intelligence.

Feel your breath and heartbeat aligning — two rhythms becoming one.
This is coherence — your body and consciousness moving in harmony.

The heart is the doorway; breath is the key.

Place one hand gently over your heart.
Sense the warmth beneath your palm — the pulse of life itself.

Now imagine the golden light within your chest expanding outward. With each breath, it grows — filling your torso, your arms, your legs. Expanding through your skin, beyond your aura, until you are surrounded by a sphere of radiant golden energy.

This is your **Heart Field** — the living field of coherence that connects you to all that is.

Breathe in — feel the field expand.
Breathe out — feel it stabilize.

Stay here until you can sense yourself surrounded by shimmering gold — calm, warm, infinite.

You are not inside the light. The light is inside you.

Now, allow the edges of your golden field to soften —
so that it begins to blend with the energy around you.

Feel the boundary between your body and the space dissolve.
The air, the room, the earth — all begin to vibrate at the same frequency.

You are no longer a single note — you are the entire symphony.
Every tree, every star, every heart is part of this radiant field of light.

This is the **Golden Field of Oneness** —
the consciousness that connects all living systems through love, coherence, and intelligent design.

You may feel warmth in your chest, tingling in your hands, or a gentle hum in your body.
These are the signatures of alignment — your field synchronizing with the universal frequency.

Here, you are infinite and intimate all at once.

In your mind or aloud, repeat softly:

"I am one with the golden field.
I am coherence in motion.
I am the medicine, the messenger, and the miracle.
I am peace remembering itself through light."

Allow these words to ripple through your field — not as language,
but as vibration.
With each repetition, your coherence strengthens and your
awareness expands.

Feel love extending from your heart into the collective —
to those you know, those you don't, to all beings, all forms, all
worlds.

Everything breathes with you.
Everything *is* you.

This is unity beyond understanding — it is knowing without thought.

Begin to bring your awareness back to your physical body —
the rise and fall of your breath,
the weight of your hands,
the stillness of your form.

Know that even as you return to ordinary consciousness,
the Golden Field remains — always present, always accessible.

You do not leave it; you carry it with you.
Every action, every word, every breath from this moment forward
radiates coherence into the world.

You are the living bridge between light and form.

As you open your eyes, take one last breath and whisper to yourself:

"I am whole.
I am light.
I am home."

And so it is.
You have entered the Golden Field of Oneness —
the space where healing, genius, and divinity converge.

May your every breath ripple coherence through the collective.
May your presence awaken harmony wherever you walk.
And may the golden field within you forever remind you:

You were never separate from the light.
You are — and have always been — the light itself.

"Gratitude is the most advanced technology for changing your vibration."

Tools & Resources

Transformation deepens when practice becomes pattern and reflection becomes awareness.

This section is designed to help you **apply**, **track**, and **expand** your coherence journey.
Use these tools before, during, and after completing the book — or integrate them into your healing practice, workshops, and professional training.

"The New Paradigm of Healing isn't about escaping technology — it's about infusing it with consciousness."

1 | Coherence Self-Assessment

(Pre- and Post-Integration Reflection)

"What we measure, we magnify."

Before you begin (and again after completing your practices), reflect honestly on the following prompts.
Circle or rate yourself from **1 (rarely true)** to **5 (always true)**.
The goal is awareness, not perfection.

Question	1 2 3 4 5

I wake up feeling calm and focused.

I can return to emotional balance quickly after stress.

I feel connected to my body and my breath.

My thoughts and emotions feel aligned rather than conflicting.

I sense my energy field or aura as strong and clear.

I can feel when I'm "in coherence."

I sense when I'm absorbing others' energy and can recalibrate easily.

Gratitude and compassion come naturally, even in challenge.

My creativity and intuition flow easily.

I feel connected to something larger than myself.

Add your total and compare it pre- and post-book.
Growth isn't linear — celebrate shifts in awareness, ease, and stability.

Remember: Coherence is not a destination, it's a rhythm you return to.

2 | Quick Reference: The 5 Phases of Transformation

A snapshot of the Zone of Healing Genius Method™

Phase	Essence	Energetic Purpose	Practice Anchor
1. Awareness	See the pattern.	Observing without judgment.	3-Minute Breath or Energy Audit
2. Acknowledgment	Name the truth.	Honesty dissolves resistance.	Emotion Recognition Practice
3. Activation	Choose the new frequency.	Intention + kinesthetic touch.	Dual-Point Touch Sequence
4. Repatterning	Rewire thought + emotion.	Replace reaction with resonance.	5-Minute Daily Repattern
5. Integration	Live as coherence.	Stabilize through repetition.	Morning & Evening Frequency Rituals

Keep this chart nearby when practicing — it's your roadmap for self-regulation, healing, and alignment.

When you know which phase you're in, you know what your energy needs.

3 | Journal & Reflection Prompts

Awareness deepens through reflection — the page becomes your mirror of coherence.

Use these prompts to anchor insight after meditations or major energetic shifts.

Daily Coherence Check-In

- What emotion dominated my energy today?
- When did I feel most in flow?
- When did I lose coherence — and how did I return?
- What frequency word describes my current state?
- What's one thing I'm grateful for that I didn't notice yesterday?

Integration Reflections

- How has my definition of "healing" evolved since starting this book?
- Which pattern have I dissolved — and which still holds a lesson for me?
- What does coherence feel like in my body, my relationships, my environment?
- How do I serve others through my coherence rather than through effort?
- What does living as "The Zone of Healing Genius" look like for me?

Your journal is not a record of progress — it's a reflection of frequency.

4 | Pattern Recognition Chart

"What you can name, you can neutralize. What you can feel, you can free."

Patterns are energetic programs — automatic loops that repeat through emotion, thought, and physical response.
Some patterns protect us, others limit us.
The key is awareness: identifying what's running in the background of your energy field so you can choose a higher frequency.

Use this chart to explore your recurring patterns across the **Four Bodies of Intelligence** — *Emotional, Mental, Physical, and Spiritual.*
Rate how strongly each one resonates with you from **1 (rarely true)** to **5 (frequently true)**, then reflect on where you feel it in your body or life.

Zone of Awareness: Identifying Your Dominant Energetic Programs

Pattern Name	Description / Common Signs	Primary Body	Frequency Range	Your Intensity (1–5)
The Healer's Wound	Always helping others while neglecting self; feels responsible for everyone's pain.	Emotional	Low Compassion → Balanced Love	
The Over-Thinker	Constant mental chatter; analyzing every detail; finds it hard to feel.	Mental	High Beta → Balanced Alpha	

Pattern Name	Description / Common Signs	Primary Body	Frequency Range	Your Intensity (1–5)
Not-Enough Program	Deep sense of inadequacy or imposter syndrome; perfectionism; overachievement.	Mental/Emotional	Low Worth → Empowered Value	
Hidden Anger	Suppressed frustration, resentment, or resistance; tight jaw, stiff shoulders, digestive tension.	Physical/Emotional	Compressed → Expressed	
Fear of Visibility	Playing small; fear of judgment or rejection; hiding true gifts.	Spiritual/Emotional	Constricted → Radiant	
The Rescuer Loop	Attracted to fixing or saving others to feel purpose; exhaustion and disappointment follow.	Emotional/Spiritual	Over-Giving → Empowered Service	

Pattern Name	Description / Common Signs	Primary Body	Frequency Range	Your Intensity (1–5)
Control Frequency	Need to plan, predict, and protect; resists surrender; discomfort with flow.	Mental	Tension → Trust	
The Doubter	Questions intuition or spiritual connection; relies solely on logic.	Mental/Spiritual	Disconnected → Aligned Knowing	
Self-Sacrifice Program	Guilt around self-care; equates rest with laziness; burnout cycle.	Physical/Emotional	Drained → Rejuvenated	
The Bypasser	Avoids deep emotion by escaping into positivity, spiritual theory, or intellect.	Spiritual	Fragmented → Integrated	

Reflection Prompts

- Which pattern scored the highest intensity?
- How long has it been present in your life?
- What emotion or belief sustains it?
- How does this pattern serve you — and what does it protect you from feeling?
- Which body (emotional, mental, physical, or spiritual) is asking for coherence?
- What *new frequency* could replace it (e.g., trust, peace, joy, self-worth)?

Recognition is the first reprogramming.
Every time you see the pattern without judgment, you raise its vibration.

Optional: AI Reflection – Pattern Recognition as Energy Data

In the **Age of AI**, our emotional and energetic patterns are like algorithms — running loops based on past data.
When you change your inner frequency, you rewrite the code.

Ask yourself:

- What "data" do I keep feeding my energy field through thoughts or emotions?
- What would my Natural Intelligence choose to upload instead?
- How can I use both technology and consciousness as mirrors for self-awareness?

Healing begins when data becomes awareness and awareness becomes energy in motion.
Each pattern you transform creates new coherence — not only in your body but in the collective field.

As you reprogram your frequency, you become the living proof of conscious evolution.

"Gratitude is the most advanced technology for changing your vibration."

5 | Chakra and Frequency Correlation Table

"Each chakra is a transmitter of consciousness — tuning it changes the frequency of your entire being."

The chakra system is the original energetic network — a living circuitry of light that mirrors the nervous system, endocrine glands, and electromagnetic field of the human body.

In the **New Paradigm of Conscious Healing**, these seven energy centers can also be understood as **frequency hubs** — each vibrating at a specific resonance measurable in both the physical and emotional spectrum.

Use this table to understand how **frequency, emotion, and coherence** work together to create healing and alignment across the four bodies of intelligence (physical, emotional, mental, spiritual).

Chakra–Frequency–Function Correlation Table

Chakra	Location & Element	Approx. Frequency (Hz)	Primary Function / Theme	Physical Correlates	Coherent State (Balanced)	Incoherent State (Imbalanced)
Root (Muladhara)	Base of spine / Earth	256 Hz (C note)	Survival, safety, stability, grounding	Adrenals, spine, legs, bones	Grounded, secure, present	Fear, insecurity, anxiety

Chakra	Location & Element	Approx. Frequency (Hz)	Primary Function / Theme	Physical Correlates	Coherent State (Balanced)	Incoherent State (Imbalanced)
Sacral (Svadhisthana)	Below navel / Water	288 Hz (D note)	Creativity, emotions, pleasure, relationships	Reproductive organs, kidneys, hips	Joy, flow, emotional intelligence	Guilt, shame, creative block
Solar Plexus (Manipura)	Upper abdomen / Fire	320 Hz (E note)	Confidence, personal power, will	Digestive system, liver, pancreas	Empowered, decisive, vibrant	Doubt, shame, lack of drive
Heart (Anahata)	Center of chest / Air	341.3 Hz (F note)	Love, compassion, forgiveness, coherence	Heart, lungs, thymus	Grateful, peaceful, connected	Grief, resentment, isolation
Throat (Vishuddha)	Throat / Ether	384 Hz (G note)	Communication, expression, truth	Thyroid, throat, mouth, shoulders	Authentic, expressive, aligned	Repressed, misunderstood, withdrawn

Chakra	Location & Element	Approx. Frequency (Hz)	Primary Function / Theme	Physical Correlates	Coherent State (Balanced)	Incoherent State (Imbalanced)
Third Eye (Ajna)	Forehead / Light	426.7 Hz (A note)	Intuition, insight, perception	Pituitary, eyes, sinuses	Clear vision, intuition, inner knowing	Confusion, overthinking, illusion
Crown (Sahasrara)	Top of head / Consciousness	480 Hz (B note)	Spiritual connection, awareness, unity	Pineal gland, brain, nervous system	Enlightened, peaceful, connected to Source	Disconnected, cynical, spiritually numb

Energetic Insight: Chakras as Frequency Gateways

Each chakra acts like a **transceiver** — sending and receiving vibrational data between your biofield and the universal field. When one center becomes over- or under-active, the entire system falls out of **coherence** — much like one instrument out of tune in an orchestra.

Coherence practices (breathwork, sound healing, kinesthetic touch, or intention-based awareness) help restore **harmonic resonance**, allowing your emotional, mental, physical, and spiritual bodies to synchronize again.

The more coherent your energy field, the clearer your intuition, creativity, and healing capacity become.

AI Reflection: Frequency Meets Technology

Modern science — especially bioresonance, neurofeedback, and AI-assisted frequency mapping — is beginning to measure what ancient healers have always known:
that **emotion = vibration,** and **frequency = information.**

- **AI can detect** patterns of stress, heart rate variability, and coherence.
- **Natural Intelligence can interpret** those signals through intuition, breath, and feeling.
  Together, they form the future of **Conscious Medicine** — where data meets divine design.

Artificial Intelligence may read your signals — but only Natural Intelligence can translate them into wisdom.

Practice Suggestion: Chakra Frequency Alignment

1. **Choose a chakra** that feels tense or disconnected.
2. **Play its resonant tone** (C–B notes listed above) or hum the sound softly.
3. **Visualize the chakra color** glowing brighter as you breathe coherence into that area.
4. **Feel the vibration** expand until it synchronizes with your heartbeat.
5. End with gratitude — your field has just re-entered harmony.

6 | Vibrational Healing Scale Chart

"Every emotion emits a frequency — and every frequency is a doorway back to coherence."

Energy is the language of healing.
Each thought, feeling, and belief produces a measurable vibration in the body's electromagnetic field.
Low-frequency states create contraction, confusion, and illness.
High-frequency states generate expansion, clarity, and healing.

This **Vibrational Healing Scale** helps you locate your current energetic state and consciously raise your frequency through coherence — the alignment of heart, mind, and soul.

Vibrational Healing Scale

Frequency Band	Vibration Level (Hz)	Emotional / Mental State	Energy Movement	Healing Focus	Practice for Elevation
Shame / Guilt	20–75 Hz	Self-blame, regret, unworthiness	Constricted / collapsing	Forgiveness, acceptance	Touch heart + breathe gratitude; affirm self-worth
Fear / Anxiety	100–150 Hz	Worry, panic, uncertainty	Erratic / fragmented	Safety, trust	Grounding breath; Root Chakra

Frequency Band	Vibration Level (Hz)	Emotional / Mental State	Energy Movement	Healing Focus	Practice for Elevation
					sound "LAM"
Anger / Resentment	150–200 Hz	Frustration, hostility, irritation	Explosive / unstable	Compassion, release	Dual-Point Touch (anger spot → heart)
Grief / Sadness	200–250 Hz	Loss, disappointment, isolation	Descending / heavy	Connection, comfort	Heart-breath coherence; imagine emerald light expanding
Apathy / Exhaustion	250–275 Hz	Hopelessness, burnout, detachment	Flat / low charge	Rejuvenation, rest	Slow rhythmic breathing; visualize gentle sunrise
Acceptance / Clarity	300–350 Hz	Calm observation, openness	Balanced / neutral	Perspective, peace	"Observe, don't absorb"

Frequency Band	Vibration Level (Hz)	Emotional / Mental State	Energy Movement	Healing Focus	Practice for Elevation
					practice; Third Eye breath
Courage / Empowerment	350–400 Hz	Confidence, motivation, readiness	Forward / activating	Action, creation	Solar Plexus breathing; visualize golden flame
Love / Compassion	400–500 Hz	Connection, harmony, care	Expanding / coherent	Unity, empathy	Heart–brain coherence breath (HeartMath method)
Gratitude / Joy	500–600 Hz	Bliss, inspiration, delight	Radiant / magnetic	Flow, vitality	Daily gratitude journaling; hands over heart

Frequency Band	Vibration Level (Hz)	Emotional / Mental State	Energy Movement	Healing Focus	Practice for Elevation
Peace / Coherence	600–700 Hz	Stillness, centeredness, trust	Resonant / harmonic	Integration, balance	Slow coherent breathing; 5-minute coherence meditation
Unity / Enlightenment	700–1000+ Hz	Oneness, illumination, compassion for all life	Omnidirectional / radiant	Pure consciousness	Golden Field of Oneness meditation

How to Use the Vibrational Healing Scale

1. **Identify:** Notice your dominant emotional or energetic state.
2. **Locate:** Find its frequency range on the chart.
3. **Acknowledge:** Feel it fully — awareness is the first step to transformation.
4. **Choose:** Select a *Practice for Elevation* to raise your vibration.
5. **Anchor:** Breathe into your heart and visualize your frequency increasing with every exhale.

The body follows the field — when your frequency rises, your biology harmonizes.

Scientific Note: Frequency and Consciousness

Studies in quantum biology and neurocardiology show that the heart's electromagnetic field changes with emotional states. Positive emotions like gratitude and love produce **coherent heart rhythms** that stabilize brain waves and support healing throughout the body.

Tesla called this the "harmonic law of vibration."
Modern science now calls it **biofield coherence** — the measurable link between frequency and physiology.

Coherence is the bridge between vibration and biology — the meeting point of science and spirit.

AI Reflection: Measuring the Invisible

In the **Age of AI**, frequency is becoming data.
Wearables now measure heart-rate variability, emotional states, and energetic output.
But technology can only record — it cannot interpret.

Artificial Intelligence can analyze your signals.
Natural Intelligence — your intuition, awareness, and compassion — gives them meaning.

Healing begins when data becomes devotion — when technology serves consciousness, not replaces it.

Energetic Insight

Every moment you choose coherence, you shift your vibration upward.
Each breath of love, gratitude, and presence recalibrates the collective field.

You don't have to chase light to heal.
You only have to stop dimming it.

7 | Daily Frequency Calibration Journal Prompts

"Healing happens each time you choose coherence over reaction."

The purpose of this daily practice is to attune your energy field — to consciously align your emotional, mental, and physical frequencies before they drift into dissonance.
Think of it as tuning your internal instrument each morning and evening so your energy plays in harmony with life.

These prompts will help you observe, recalibrate, and elevate your vibration day by day.
Use them in your journal or within your digital tracking app.
They are your moment of reflection — your daily meeting between *Natural Intelligence and conscious awareness.*

Morning Calibration: Setting the Frequency

"Your morning energy sets the tone for your entire field."

1. What frequency am I waking up in today?
(List a word, color, or sensation that describes your current vibration — e.g., heavy, open, scattered, peaceful.)

2. Which emotion or thought loop seems to be leading my energy?
(Awareness turns unconscious patterns into data you can shift.)

3. What vibration do I want to cultivate today?
(Choose one coherent frequency: peace, gratitude, clarity, joy, courage, or love.)

4. Which body—physical, emotional, mental, or spiritual—needs the most care right now?
(This focuses your practice where alignment is needed.)

5. What single action, breath, or thought can bring me into coherence this morning?
(Keep it simple: a breath sequence, gratitude focus, or moment of stillness.)

"Set your vibration before the world sets it for you."

Evening Calibration: Closing the Field

"Every night, coherence restores what the mind cannot fix."

1. When today did I feel most in coherence?
(Notice the sensations — warmth, stillness, expansion, peace — these are your signature frequency markers.)

2. When did I lose coherence, and what triggered it?
(Gently name the emotion or situation; avoid judgment — awareness is healing.)

3. How did I return to balance, or what could I have done differently?
(Reflect on which phase of the Zone of Healing Genius Method™ helped you.)

4. What frequency am I carrying into rest tonight?
(Write one word to summarize your energy — e.g., calm, gratitude, renewal.)

5. How can I elevate my vibration before sleep?
(Heart-breathing, visualization, or simply whispering your chosen frequency.)

"Sleep becomes sacred when coherence leads you into it."

Weekly Reflection Prompts

At the end of each week, review your entries and ask:

- Which frequency did I visit most often?
- What patterns pulled me out of coherence?
- What practices or environments amplified my energy the most?
- How is my external world mirroring my internal vibration?
- What evidence of transformation have I noticed in my relationships, health, or creativity?

Your journal becomes a mirror of your evolution — a record of energy becoming consciousness.

AI Reflection: Tracking the Invisible

You can enhance this practice by integrating technology consciously:

- Use a **heart-rate variability (HRV) app** or **biofeedback wearable** to monitor physiological coherence.
- Note how your emotional reflections correlate with your recorded data.
- Let **Artificial Intelligence** reveal the data — but let **Natural Intelligence** interpret the meaning.

When your heart's rhythm and your awareness align, you become your own calibration device.

Energetic Insight

Journaling is frequency medicine. Each word anchors vibration into form. Each reflection tunes your energy closer to coherence. *You don't write to remember — you write to realign.*

"The future of healing won't be human versus machine — it will be a symphony. Technology will measure energy, but consciousness will conduct it. The real genius is learning how to stay coherent in both worlds."

"We are entering an age where frequency is language, and coherence is power."

Bibliography

Where science and spirit meet — the research, resonance, and remembrance behind coherence.

ENERGY & BIOFIELD SCIENCE

- Hunt, V. P. (1996). *Infinite Mind: Science of the Human Vibrations of Consciousness.* Malibu Publishing.
- Oschman, J. L. (2016). *Energy Medicine: The Scientific Basis.* Elsevier.
- Rubik, B., Hahn, J., & Royal, R. (2002). *The Biofield Hypothesis: Energy Medicine and the Human Body. Journal of Alternative and Complementary Medicine*, 8(6), 703–717.
- Gerber, R. (2001). *Vibrational Medicine: The #1 Handbook of Subtle-Energy Therapies.* Bear & Company.
- Shealy, C. N., & Myss, C. (1993). *The Creation of Health: The Emotional, Psychological, and Spiritual Responses That Promote Healing.* Stillpoint Publishing.

HEART–BRAIN COHERENCE & EMOTION RESEARCH

- McCraty, R. (2015). *Science of the Heart: Exploring the Role of the Heart in Human Performance.* HeartMath Institute.
- Childre, D., & Martin, H. (1999). *The HeartMath Solution: The Institute of HeartMath's Revolutionary Program for Engaging the Power of the Heart's Intelligence.* HarperOne.
- Pearsall, P. (1998). *The Heart's Code: Tapping the Wisdom and Power of Our Heart Energy.* Broadway Books.
- Pert, C. B. (1997). *Molecules of Emotion: The Science Behind Mind–Body Medicine.* Scribner.

CONSCIOUSNESS, FLOW, AND RESONANCE

- Csikszentmihalyi, M. (1990). *Flow: The Psychology of Optimal Experience.* Harper & Row.
- Dispenza, J. (2017). *Becoming Supernatural: How Common People Are Doing the Uncommon.* Hay House.
- Tiller, W. A., Dibble, W. E., & Kohane, M. J. (2001). *Conscious Acts of Creation: The Emergence of a New Physics.* Pavior Publishing.
- Bohm, D. (1980). *Wholeness and the Implicate Order.* Routledge.
- McGilchrist, I. (2010). *The Master and His Emissary: The Divided Brain and the Making of the Western World.* Yale University Press.

FREQUENCY, WATER & EMOTION

- Emoto, M. (2004). *The Hidden Messages in Water.* Beyond Words Publishing.
- Schafer, W. (2011). *Energy Healing for Beginners.* Llewellyn Publications.
- Lipton, B. H. (2005). *The Biology of Belief: Unleashing the Power of Consciousness, Matter & Miracles.* Hay House.
- Becker, R. O., & Selden, G. (1998). *The Body Electric: Electromagnetism and the Foundation of Life.* Harper.

INTEGRATION & FUTURE MEDICINE

- Dossey, L. (2009). *The Power of Premonitions: How Knowing the Future Can Shape Our Lives.* Dutton.
- Chopra, D. (1989). *Quantum Healing: Exploring the Frontiers of Mind/Body Medicine.* Bantam Books.
- McTaggart, L. (2008). *The Field: The Quest for the Secret Force of the Universe.* HarperCollins.

- Laszlo, E. (2004). *Science and the Akashic Field: An Integral Theory of Everything.* Inner Traditions.
- Schwartz, G. E., & Russek, L. G. S. (1999). *The Living Energy Universe.* Hampton Roads.

ADDITIONAL INSPIRATIONAL AND FOUNDATIONAL WORKS

- Tesla, N. (1900). *The Problem of Increasing Human Energy. Century Illustrated Magazine.*
- Robbins, T. (1991). *Awaken the Giant Within.* Simon & Schuster.
- Graziosi, D. (2019). *Millionaire Success Habits: The Gateway to Wealth and Prosperity.* Hay House.
- Santego, C. (2025). *The Zone of Healing Genius.* Maximillian Enterprises.

Message From The Author

The greatest medicine we can offer the world is our own coherence."

When I first began studying energy medicine more than two decades ago, I thought I was learning separate systems — Reiki, chakras, vibrational science, emotional release, Tesla frequencies, and spiritual psychology. Each modality felt like a unique doorway into healing. But as I kept walking through them, I discovered they all led to the same luminous center — **the intelligence of coherence.**

That realization changed everything. Healing stopped being something I *did* and became something I *allowed.* It was never about fixing what was broken. It was about remembering the natural harmony that exists beneath the noise — the field where the heart, mind, and soul speak the same language of frequency.

Writing *The new paradigm: Conscious Healing In The Age Of Ai* has been the culmination of that lifelong exploration. It's my way of offering back to the collective what I've witnessed in countless students and clients: that transformation is not found in complexity, but in returning to simplicity — one breath, one thought, one touch at a time.

We are entering an extraordinary era. Artificial intelligence is advancing rapidly, revealing how much can be analyzed, predicted, and automated. Yet, as I've written throughout this book, **it is our natural intelligence that holds the power to heal, love, and evolve.** Technology may simulate thinking, but only the human heart can create coherence. Only the living, breathing field of consciousness can sense truth, compassion, and connection.

My hope is that this work reminds you that you are not separate from the intelligence that designed you. You are its expression — a pulse of creation moving through human form.

Every time you choose to breathe deeply, to feel instead of resist, to harmonize instead of react, you are reprogramming the field — not just for yourself, but for all who share it.

You are the medicine.
You are the messenger.
You are the miracle.

Thank you for walking this path with me — for trusting that science and soul can belong in the same conversation, that healing is both measurable and mystical, and that coherence is the future of medicine and consciousness.

May this book serve as both map and mirror — helping you remember the brilliance that was never lost, only waiting to be seen again.

With love, gratitude, and golden light,
Dr. Constance Santego, Ph.D., DNM
Natural Medicine Doctor | Grand Reiki Master | Author & Teacher of Conscious Healing

About the Author

Dr. Constance Santego, Ph.D., DNM, is an award-winning author, natural medicine doctor, and internationally respected teacher of energy healing and consciousness studies. For more than twenty-five years, she has dedicated her life to helping others awaken their innate capacity to heal — emotionally, mentally, physically, and spiritually.

A Grand Reiki Master and founder of multiple wellness and educational programs, Dr. Santego has trained thousands of students worldwide in Reiki, vibrational healing, and intuitive development. Her groundbreaking teachings unite ancient wisdom with modern science, revealing how frequency, intention, and coherence can reshape both the body and the mind.

Through her books, courses, and speaking engagements, she brings to life the principle that **healing is not about fixing what's broken, but remembering what's whole.** Her work bridges the gap between traditional healing arts and emerging scientific research on the biofield, consciousness, and heart–brain coherence.

Dr. Santego is the author of more than forty published works — including the *Reiki Wisdom* series, the *Secrets of a Healer* guides, and her acclaimed spiritual fiction series on *The Nine Spiritual Gifts.* Her publications have become cornerstones for students and practitioners seeking a deeper understanding of holistic and energy-based medicine.

She lives in beautiful British Columbia, Canada, where she continues to write, teach, and inspire others to live in their highest vibration — grounded in love, aligned in coherence, and guided by purpose.

"My mission is to merge science and spirit — to remind humanity that the most advanced technology on Earth is the human heart."

ALSO AVAILABLE

For additional information on

Constance Santego's

wide range of Motivational Products, Coaching Sessions, Spiritual Retreats,
Live Events and Educational Programs

Go to

www.ConstanceSantego.ca

Follow on Instagram - Constance_Santego and
Facebook - constancesantegoo

Subscribe and receive Free Information and Meditations on her
YouTube Channel - Constance Santego

Secrets of a Healer, Magic of Reiki

ISBN: 978-1-7772220-0-0

Secrets of a Healer, The Reiki Master's Manual

ISBN: 978-1-990062-34-6

www.ingramcontent.com/pod-product-compliance
Lightning Source LLC
Chambersburg PA
CBHW071719120626
46550CB00001B/302